MARK T. BARCLAY

GOD

POSSESSED

God Possessed
ISBN 978-0-944802-60-1
Copyright © 2017 Mark T. Barclay

Published by Mark Barclay Publications
Mark Barclay Ministries
2010 N. Stark Road, Midland, MI 48642-9439
www.marktbarclay.com

2010 N. Stark Road • Midland, MI 48642-9439

CONTENTS

INTRODUCTION

It was a typical winter day in Michigan—very cold, fairly windy, and with a boatload of snow. I was out and about in the city where I lived and actually ran into an old school friend. As we reminisced of days gone by, we also began to share about our lives now. I was free, and he was still horribly bound to alcohol. I was prosperous, and he was still suffering under terrible poverty. I was happy, and he explained how he was living a life of depression. He made a statement to me referring to my Christian life and said, "Well, Mark, you just got religion and it worked for you, I guess." My answer came swiftly and sharp as a two-edged sword: "I did not get religion. I met a person called Jesus Christ, and since that moment of time all evil has left me, and all evil shackles have been torn away from my life. Religion is nothing more than a list of do's and don'ts, with absolutely no power to do the do's or stop doing the don'ts." That very conversation inspired me to begin to tell my story to the entire world. I'm doing that more and more now as I preach, teach, pastor, and write.

I am writing this book for three reasons. First of all, I'm writing it for the multitude of people who may read it and learn from it that if God can use Mark Barclay, God can use anybody. I pray that as you read through the entire thing, you will discover that no matter how small a village you come from, how insignificant you think you are, how small you believe your name may be, or how impossible your future looks to you, there is a God in Heaven, and He has a plan for you.

I am also writing this book because my five fathers in the faith— Dr. Lester Sumrall, Dr. John Osteen, Dr. Roy Hicks, Dr. George Evans, and Dr. Hilton Sutton—continually told me that I must put my story on paper so others can pull strength from it. Because I was a submitted man while they were all living on this earth and actively involved in my life and ministry, I have decided to go ahead and continue to be submitted to their counsel.

Third, I'm writing this book for my family—Vickie, my beautiful bride of many years; my daughter Dawn and her husband James; my son Josh and his wife Trish; and my grandchildren—as well as for a multitude of great believers and people from around the world who have asked me if I have ever written a book solely based on my own life story and have encouraged me to do this work.

My prayer is that as you read this book, it will not just be my story but a motivator and a great inspiration, adding to the elements of your life that make you an earth warrior and a great giant slayer.

At all costs, at all times, obey God! As John Osteen once said to me, "I've learned one thing if I've learned anything about this life, and that is that God knows more than John."

May the great Holy Spirit touch you and put His finger upon something in your heart so that my life of chasing our God can somehow be of value to you. I have shared some of my favorite verses and greatest secrets, as well as some very precious stories… all to the glory of our God!

1

PERPETUAL MOTION

**PREPARING GOD'S PEOPLE FOR HIS COMING
WITH EVERY MEANS AVAILABLE TO US BY GOD**

Ever since I met Vickie Lynn St. Dennis at age 13 in 1965 and marrying her in 1970, we have been in this perpetual motion, which we call "our life." And this perpetual motion has greatly intensified since meeting our Lord, Jesus Christ.

Without exaggeration, I have walked hundreds of miles, driven thousands of miles, and flown millions of miles in decades of service to reach a hurting, suffering, lost, troubled world. I have crossed every ocean and stood on every continent. I have climbed mountains, floated down rivers, dredged through swamps, and survived the hottest deserts of the world. From the greatest metropolises to the smallest villages, from the natives of the jungle to the most educated and intelligent in the skyscrapers of our major cities, I have preached to the multitudes in the morning and flown to a faithful dozen believers at night. Men and women of all cultures, languages, and religions have heard my voice and seen my face.

I am Mark T. Barclay, disciple of Christ and missionary, reaching the unreached and telling the untold, and this is my story!

2

IF ONLY CARS COULD TALK

If cars could talk, you should start visiting the junkyards to find all the old cars I have driven into the ground while traveling for Jesus Christ and listen to the wild, Holy Ghost stories they would tell you about each trip. In fact, visit the airplane boneyards as well.

Many times God Almighty has spoken to me while driving along on a mission to help a pastor and his church, or to preach at a campmeeting, or to speak at a leadership conference. If they could talk, one of my old, worn-out cars would tell you how many young preachers I have raised up by spending day after day with them in a car as we traveled together across the country.

If canoes and small handcrafted boats could speak, they would tell you how many times they heard us sing unto God while swatting malaria-infested mosquitoes or using our faith to ward off the threat of the wary native.

If animals could talk, they would tell you some of the greatest secrets of survival and conquest as they were the beast of burden that carried my team and me from one desolate place to another, all the time hearing us speak to God in our heavenly tongues.

If trees and bushes could talk, they would want you to take some hikes across rugged terrain such as is found on the Pacific Islands or in the jungles of Africa or the outback and mountains of South America. They would tell you how we cried out to God to stay strong (and alive!) to preach the gospel of Jesus Christ, sometimes to just a handful of people.

If airplanes could just talk, any of the aircraft our ministry has flown since 1982 would tell you many of my greatest secrets and those of some of the greatest men and women of God who were on board as we jetted to meeting after meeting. Some of the deepest revelations God has given me came in the dark of the night, at high altitude, when it was just God and me, conversing and sharing deep inner secrets with each other.

Each one of those airplanes could testify of my right living and my attention to spiritual things. If they could just talk, they would tell you how many hours were spent fellowshipping with Jesus, and how many hours were spent praying in tongues while soaring through the sky at hundreds of miles an hour. They would tell you how many times I took off from a meeting and wept most of the way home because the pastor or the people were hurting so badly, or the times we laughed together (the Lord and I) as we rejoiced over what He did in the meetings and the many people who were helped, healed, or delivered.

If airplanes, motor vehicles, and animals could talk, they would testify to the fact that there was always a Bible open and people praying on every trip I have ever made. They would tell you the multitude of times I have looked to Heaven, and with a swollen heart of gratitude thanked God for using me in any way to do anything, because I have always felt inadequate and insufficient to fulfill His assignments.

You may not know me personally, but if you could ever talk to any one of the young men, pilots, armorbearers, security personnel, or family members who live around me, they would tell you there has never been any sin, cheating, lying, carnality, booze, drugs, gossip, or slander in our lives or ministry or any such blemish that would dirty our walk with God or quench our anointing.

Though I am now a God-possessed man, my life didn't start out that way. The following chapters will prove to you there exists a saving, delivering Christ who can take a loser and worldly earthling like Mark Timothy Barclay and make him an obedient servant of the Most High God and use him to reach multitudes of people globally. If you really knew the old Mark Barclay, you would be encouraged that if God can use him, He can use anyone!

3

NOT ME, LORD

GENESIS 32:10

I am not worthy of the least of all the mercies, and of all the truth, which thou hast shewed unto thy servant…

1 SAMUEL 9:21

And Saul answered and said, *Am* not I a Benjamite, of the smallest of the tribes of Israel? and my family the least of all the families of the tribe of Benjamin? wherefore then speakest thou so to me?

JUDGES 6:15

And he said unto him, Oh my Lord, wherewith shall I save Israel? behold, my family *is* poor in Manasseh, and I *am* the least in my father's house.

I have never felt as qualified as my preaching comrades and colleagues seem to be. I do not fight an actual inferiority complex or a poor self-image. I do not condemn myself, and I do not belittle myself. I have chosen to say what God says over me and about me.

However, I have always been blown away at how God has spoken to me and by the many things He has entrusted to me. To this day I am still somewhat bewildered that God could and would use someone like me—someone with no famous family and from no famous place, someone with no true spiritual roots, a young man with no pastor to follow, someone born poor and raised poor.

All these years I have told the Lord Jesus, "I am a soldier, and I will obey You at all costs. Command me, and I will obey. I am Yours to command. But are You sure I am the right man for this assignment?"

I actually don't remember a time in decades of service to my King that I ever received an assignment or mission that was easy or that wouldn't take a miracle or chain of miracles to accomplish. I don't ever remember thinking that any assignment would be easy or a no-sweat assignment. They all seemed so impossible to me.

I remember Gloria Copeland (whom Vickie and I love dearly) once saying that she told Kenneth that if the assignments God gave them were not impossible to man, anyone could do them. She said, "They were given to us because we walk with the God of the impossible."

Don't misunderstand me here. I am an earth warrior to the maximum degree. I am thoroughly trained and fully equipped by God to conquer. I have supernatural weapons and armor. I speak with a supernatural language that only God can interpret; it is a mystery to all humans. I am washed by the blood of the Lamb, and I bear the name of Jesus. I have the Bible as my sword, and I believe it in my heart and hurl it out of my mouth toward the enemy, and it knocks the devil and his army of invisible enemy soldiers out of my way.

I am not at all saying that I am weak or scared. No, I am saying that on the inside I have always felt like I could not win without full obedience to God's Word and full submission to Him. I am very disciplined and have always had more than enough courage when needed. I am very bold, but it is all in Christ. May I decrease, and may He increase in my life and ministry (John 3:30).

While growing up I never knew what pride was, though I was probably full of it. They say that pride is one of those things you don't know you have, but everyone around you knows. Besides, I was filled with every other stupid, dark, and evil thing. It was later on, after I became a Christian, that I understood the difference between pride and humility.

I still remember clearly my call to preach and how I felt so inadequate and at first said no to God. I actually said, "Not me, Lord—You've got the wrong man!" (I will tell that story later in the book.) Most great men and women of God whom Vickie and I have ever met were humble gospel workers and knew they must depend totally on God to finish their course on this earth.

I could tell stories here forever about every order Heaven has ever given me and how, when I received the command, I had no faith for it and no money in the bank. Yet everything I have put my hand to that God has assigned to me has prospered.

I was blessed to have five fathers in the faith who creased my life forever. One man told me that I was very blessed to have had them and that God must have really honored me to be able to have a personal relationship with each of them (more on this matter later). I agree, but I never quite viewed it that way. I always felt that God knew I would need that much help and input, so He made sure I was well led and well covered.

Dr. George Evans was one of those fathers, and though sometimes I don't always recall which father taught me what, I believe it was Dr. Evans who often said, "The way *up* in this Kingdom is *down* on your knees." He made me into a man of constant prayer.

To this day I still find myself saying to the Lord, "Are You sure You want *me* to do that for You?" I figure if God can use a former sinner boy and former loser like me, He can use anybody.

After decades of service and obedience to the King of Glory, Jesus Christ, I still feel little on the inside and don't go an hour without touching Him and staying submitted to Him and His power. I look back over my life, and I am humbled and blown away at all God has used me to do… and I'm not finished yet! Hallelujah!

4

BORN POOR, RAISED POOR, POOR NO MORE

I MET "LITTLE BIT"

It is amazing just what part of our childhood stays with us and what things we remember. I grew up in a small village in Northern Michigan with my parents, Francis Royal and Lennah Dale Barclay. We lived next to a small inland lake, and my grandfather sold worms for fish bait and rented boats to fishermen. My dad cut tall timbers and dragged them out of the big cedar swamps with Clydesdale horses. They were then used for log cabin buildings and for poles, such as school football field lights and power company lines. I remember taking a tool called a drawshave and busting the bark off cedar poles that my dad had cut from the cedar swamps and then preparing them for fencing and other uses.

I was reminded of this not too long ago when I was visiting a fellow minister who lives in a modern log cabin-type home. Wow, what a difference a few decades make! His log cabin home is beautiful, extremely well built, and totally weatherproof. I was there during the winter, and it was very warm and well insulated.

Our house was a small log cabin, with a very small living room and two bedrooms, heated only by a wood stove. One bedroom was my parents', and the other was for the four Barclay boys. I recall an extremely small kitchen and the table with four old, wooden chairs. We had an outhouse for a bathroom and an outdoor pump for water.

I remember waking up on those cold winter mornings when snow had blown through the cracks of some of those logs and actually made little snowdrifts across the blankets over my legs. Somehow my dad always seemed to have food for us, and my mom kept us warm. When you're small and young you don't realize what a price your parents are paying to take care of you.

I have included photos of a drawshave and a little log cabin very similar to ours:

LOG CABIN SIMILAR TO MY CHILDHOOD HOME
I REMEMBER THE SNOW BLOWING BETWEEN THE LOGS
ONTO MY BED

A DRAWSHAVE... I SKINNED HUNDREDS OF LOGS

When I was around 8 years old, my dad began to get sick, and by the time I was 12, he was gone. The day my dad died, a horrible anger—a hatred for humans—came into my life, and I became a very vicious, short-tempered, and violent young man. I will share more on this in a future chapter because I believe my freedom from this driving force will help many other people find victory over tantrums, rage, and deep inner anger.

It was during these very troubled young years of my life that I met an evil spirit that I have since named "little bit." I discovered later as I became a student of the Bible that this demon is really called "poverty." That's right, the *spirit* of poverty.

One of my fathers in the faith was Dr. Lester Sumrall. I remember his teaching me about this evil spirit. I learned more from Dr. Sumrall about the spirit realm than any classes I've ever attended and any scriptures I have studied on my own. He was an absolute guru and master in the knowledge of angels and demons and how they interact in our lives. If you read the following verses, it will make better sense to you when I explain what Dr. Sumrall revealed to me about those of us who were ever bound in severe poverty.

MATTHEW 6:24

No man can serve two masters: for either he will hate the one, and love the other; or else he will hold to the one, and despise the other. Ye cannot serve God and mammon.

As the Lord began to reveal to me who these demons were and the detailed description of them, the whole spirit world opened up to me, and I began to see and understand things no one had ever taught me before. This has been so vital to my success in life. It is worthy of my writing a book on that subject alone.

Mammon was called a "master" by Jesus Christ. He clearly said that you cannot serve master mammon and Master Jesus at the same time. As I studied this more deeply, I began to see that mammon is not just treasury and currency or what modern man calls money. It is a spiritual force. Mammon wants you and me to submit to it and its system. Jesus Christ wants us to submit to Him and His kingdom.

Mammon is made up of five demons. They will chase you all of your life because the world's system is built on bartering and trading. All of us must have some form of money to operate, and many of us have been taught that the more money we have, the better we are—which is easily proven wrong. I have even heard many preachers teach that possessions are proof that one person is more spiritual than someone who doesn't have as much. They are referring to mammon as money, treasury, and possessions. Obviously they are mostly incorrect.

Before I continue, I want to declare to you that I do not at all believe in the idea that you are a lesser person or less spiritual if you find yourself in poverty's snare. Humans are funny. They always call it "dirt poor" or "filthy rich," not just poor or rich. Being raised in this dirt poverty, I can tell you firsthand that there is not one good thing about it! I will confront you if you try to convince me that being poor is being close to God or that being rich is being far from God.

So which is it? Are riches a sign of God's blessing, or are they the trap of satan? I tell you that riches, whether you have them or not, are not a sign of your spirituality. Many very evil and wicked people are among the richest people on this planet. However, how much you "love" money and how you use it will define your character for sure. Money is not alive. It has no volition. When in the hands of the wicked, it does wicked things; but in the hands of the righteous, it accomplishes righteous things.

The five demons that make up mammon are poverty, debt, lack, lust, and greed. I will only briefly touch on each of these, though it is in my heart to teach on them thoroughly. I have been recently teaching among the churches about this demon I call "little bit" and what you and I are to do about it.

THE SPIRIT OF POVERTY

Poverty is more than a lack of money. <u>Poverty is a demon</u> that will bring false teaching and literally indoctrinate you, convincing you that you are nobody, you are nothing, and therefore you can never get ahead. A poverty demon will even teach this to the rich. I know several rich people who seem to be totally bound by this poverty demon. Though they have plenty of money, they are so tight and miserly that their money haunts them instead of enhancing them. They truly are poverty-minded. Poverty haunts them night and day with the fear of not having their money and having to submit to a lower lifestyle.

THE SPIRIT OF DEBT

<u>The spirit of debt is a demon</u>. Debt is not so much borrowing but overextending oneself. Everybody knows it's much wiser to never borrow at any time. The spirit of debt will cause you to not keep your word with the lender. It will even work with the spirit of lust to cause you to buy everything your beady little eyes see, or with the spirit of lack to stop that job of yours by closing down your factory, causing you to be unemployed with no way to pay your debtor. Then you become a slave to your debtor. Terrible!

THE SPIRIT OF LACK

Simply said, <u>the spirit of lack is a demon</u>. This evil spirit of lack causes things to be withheld from you. This demon will do everything in its power to postpone your blessing, your raise, your bonus, and people just wanting to bless you. There are millions and millions of dollars of inheritance money still stored up, waiting to be distributed to the rightful heirs. However, this demon constantly creates difficulties to prevent this from happening.

The spirit of lack will do everything in its power to cause your stuff to wear out early, be stolen, be misplaced, break down, burn out, and fall apart. Isn't it amazing how many things wear out or break down just a few days after the manufacturer's warranty has expired? When this demon was bound by God in the wilderness for 40 years, the Israelites' shoes never wore out!

THE SPIRIT OF LUST

The spirit of lust is a demon that constantly works on your human lust. In the Book of James, the Bible talks about how every man is drawn away from the Word of God, the things of God, and the presence of God by his own lust. We know that the old human nature has lust within itself, and it will search after and probably never be satisfied until it conquers the thing it so deeply wants. However, there's a *spirit* of lust, a demon that serves on the board of its master, mammon, and wants you to be a servant to it. Its work is called a stronghold, an addiction, or bondage.

THE SPIRIT OF GREED

The spirit of greed is a demon that will teach you that enough is never enough. This demon will teach you to keep grabbing more and more and more and never be satisfied at any point in your life. You can see how the demon of greed and these other demons on the committee of their master, mammon, work closely together to ruin our lives and keep us under their thumb.

Though I would love to expound more clearly on these other demons, I am led by the Spirit to tell you more about their boss, the spirit of poverty. It is mammon's chairman of the board. I met that demon as a young man, and I submitted to it all of my young life until a man of God taught me how to break its power. Ever since having beaten it, I have never lived in poverty. Once you whip the demon that is behind poverty, you will more easily beat poverty.

Following is the perfect set of verses to reveal who this rascal really is:

2 KINGS 4:1-7 NIV *(original version © 1973)*

v. 1   The wife of a man from the company of the prophets cried out to Elisha, "Your servant my husband is dead, and you know that he revered the LORD. But now his creditor is coming to take my two boys as his slaves."

v. 2   Elisha replied to her, "How can I help you? Tell me, what do you have in your house?" "Your servant has nothing there at all," she said, "except a little oil."

v. 3   Elisha said, "Go around and ask all your neighbors for empty jars. Don't ask for just a few.

v. 4   Then go inside and shut the door behind you and your sons. Pour oil into all the jars, and as each is filled, put it to one side."

v. 5   She left him and afterward shut the door behind her and her sons. They brought the jars to her and she kept pouring.

v. 6   When all the jars were full, she said to her son, "Bring me another one." But he replied, "There is not a jar left." Then the oil stopped flowing.

v. 7   She went and told the man of God, and he said, "Go, sell the oil and pay your debts. You and your sons can live on what is left."

We must take a closer look at this passage and pull some very important points from it:

1. Verse 1 tells us that this widow's husband was a servant to the prophet.

2. We see that he revered the Lord.

3. We know they were in horrible debt because now in his death the creditors are coming to enslave her sons to pay the bill. If you have ever met the demon of slavery, you would know that these boys would have never been returned to their mama, even after the debt was totally paid.

4. Verse 2 shows us exactly how this sneaky, demobilizing, demoralizing demon works in one's life. When the prophet of God asked her what he could do to help her, he also asked her what she had in her house. This seems to be exactly opposite of what we do today. When someone is in great need today, the preacher usually says to wait while he goes to see what's in God's house. But this prophet asked the widow what was in *her* house.

I want you to pay very close attention to how she answered him: "Your servant has *nothing there at all,*" she said, "except a little oil." So which is it? It can't be nothing at all *and* a little bit at the same time. Either you have nothing, or you have something, even though that something is just a little bit. This is not just a play on words. This particular version of the Scriptures really points out to us how this demon indoctrinates your mind.

This demon actually taught this woman to lead with a lie or at least an inaccurate statement. She actually did have a little bit of oil at home. I've seen this spirit do the same thing to many people today. It literally teaches them that because they do not have a lot and all they have is a little bit, they must be worthless. "What could I do," they say, "with just so little?" Many people calculate that they have nothing because they don't have plenty. You can hear people speak the language of this demon.

The kingdom of God is set up on you and me getting things to the Almighty God, and in doing so it initiates a river of supply toward us. This demon wants you to come to the house of God for a handout rather than come to the house of God with a hand*ful*. Again, this is not a play on words.

As I was raised in such deep poverty, I was treated as if I wasn't smart. I guess people thought we must be dumb or dirty or misfits because we did not have plenty. I even remember being bypassed in school sports because my family was poor. A coach once said, when they were deciding on who should play first string, that they should play Barclay because he runs the ball so well, but they couldn't because another boy's dad paid for the goalposts.

I also noticed growing up that when you are poor, other people often look down on you. I'm not sure why that is, but I am poor no more, and I have never done that to other people, and I never will.

"Little bit" taught this widow that because she only had a little bit of oil, she really had nothing. This demon will do the same thing to you. I've seen it many times. Poverty will postpone you. Poverty will strip you of your energy. Poverty robs you of your confidence. This evil spirit and all the spirits of mammon must be bound, in Jesus' name.

The Bible consistently instructs us how to deal with these evil spirits:

1. Give no place to the devil.
2. Give to God so you can receive.
3. Tithe so the devourer is rebuked on your behalf.

DIRIAN'S

Dirian Grocery was a corner store in the small village where we lived. Mrs. Dirian owned and operated it. My mom would go there for whatever food and basic supplies she had enough money to buy. At this time my dad was very sick and became sick unto death. My mom did what she could to raise a few dollars to feed us four boys.

DIRIAN'S STORE (REMODELED), WHERE MY MOM SHOPPED

I remember how my mom would patiently store up dimes and quarters until she had enough to go to this store. Whenever we went to Dirian's, she would tell us four Barclay boys to not even get out of the car. She would say, "I only have enough money to get a few things. There is no reason for you boys to get out of the car." I cannot tell you how many times I heard this same speech. It was one of my mother's most worthless speeches!

My mom would pull that car into the gravel parking lot, and before the wheels were totally done turning, the four Barclay boys would go racing out of the car, headed for the store. We ran down the aisles, dodging customers and even knocking a thing or two off the shelves once in a while. We would run and stand at the end of the counter, one behind the other.

Today, we normally pass by the cashier as we pay for our items, but in those days the cashier stood behind the counter and faced you. Behind the cashier's counter at Dirian's were rows of candies, and the bottom two rows were always penny candies. Yes, that's right—*penny* candies.

We always ran to the end of the counter where Mrs. Dirian would enter through a couple saloon-type swinging doors to her workplace there at the cash register. The reason we stood there is that Mrs. Dirian would let each of us brothers step through the door, one at a time, and she would pick us up, grunt a little bit (for effect), and set us down. She would then guestimate our weight and tell us to fill our little pockets with penny candies. When we were done, she would once again "weigh" us by that same method and then charge my mom accordingly. I grew up feeling like we were always ripping off this woman because I'm not sure she really ever charged my mom much money (if any). But believe me, to a very poor kid that candy was a real treat!

CHRISTMAS AND POVERTY

Christmas was always my most exciting time of the year (and actually still is). It started for us around mid-August when the Christmas catalogs came out and were delivered in the mail to our house. (If you're under 40, let me explain what a catalog is… it is a book made of paper and ink with pictures and descriptions of the items you can buy.) We flipped through the pages manually (this was way before the Internet), and we would pick out what we wanted for our Christmas present. I remember receiving catalogs from Sears, Roebuck & Company; J.C. Penney; Montgomery Ward (which we called monkey ward); and Spiegel. I'm sure there were more, but these are the ones I remember. Each evening after we got off the school bus and did our chores, the four Barclay boys would sit down and search diligently through those catalogs, trying to decide what we wanted for a Christmas gift. You see, when you are really poor, you only get one gift, but it may not be the exact one you wished for because it all related to the cost and how much money Mom could squeeze out.

After a day or so we started to cut out of the catalog a picture of the item we chose and went to show Mom and Dad, which eventually went to just Mom. She would always act very excited and encourage us to keep looking. She knew very well that we would change our minds many times before Christmas actually came. By Christmas Eve, there was little left of those catalogs—two covers and the girls' section!

I clearly remember that one year I wanted a pair of coveralls like my grandpa wore. When my dad got so sick and eventually died, my grandpa helped raise us. It was good. He was a good, hardworking farmer. There is nowhere better to raise four hellion boys than a good, old-fashioned farm.

I called Grandpa's coveralls "farmer pants." They were actually bib overalls. He always wore blue ones. (Until I was a teenager I didn't know they came in any other colors.) I wanted a pair so badly. I told my mom that above all else I needed a pair of farmer pants, just like Grandpa's.

She tried to talk me out of it. "You don't want those," she said. "Your brothers will all have a toy, and you won't." I told her I didn't care, that it was exactly what I wanted. This went on for days as we sat around the old wood stove and showed Mom the catalog clippings (well, sometimes they were "rippings").

I finally broke her down. Christmas morning came, and we all ran to the tree. Each of us had a big gift and a couple smaller things. I was so afraid that mine wasn't going to be those farmer pants. I opened my present last. As I watched my three brothers open theirs, I kept glancing at my mom, and she seemed nervous for me. When my turn came, I opened my present… and lo and behold, there they were—my farmer pants!

I strutted around in them like I was the biggest guy in that room. They were just like my grandpa's (only significantly smaller). Every time I would sit by one of my brothers, they would scorn and tease me and say, "Get away from me, farmer," and they would play with their toys. But that was okay. I slept in them that night. Me, in my bib overalls, just like Grandpa's—wow! It's amazing how my brothers just wouldn't let that go. They kept on teasing me and calling me names like farmer in the dell, cattleman, sod buster… and worse. But that was okay because…

THEN DIRIAN DAY CAME

Mama counted up her hard-earned money and scribbled on her pad of paper, just like always, to see what she could buy and what she must leave off the list. We got our regular "don't get out of the car" lecture that we always got just before departure to the corner store. It was just as worthless and ineffective that day as it was all the days before. That car barely stopped, and off we were, headed for the swinging doors at the end of Mrs. Dirian's counter. Same routine, leaving car doors open and bumping into a customer or two and surely knocking at least a couple things off the shelf.

But today things had changed! I was first in line. When Mrs. Dirian pushed open those swinging doors and saw my bibs, her eyes got so big. She knew she'd been had. My brothers had a five-level fire alarm shock when they realized the value of those farmer pants. In fact, on future Dirian days they always treated me very well. Hey, just in case you haven't seen any lately, bibs don't just have pockets—they *are* pockets.

Back to "little bit." I first recognized him here, at Dirian's. As I was behind the counter with Mrs. Dirian, filling my pockets, I would look up to the counter, and from that view I could see my mama's face. She looked so worried and scared. I would watch her as Mrs. Dirian added up the items, and my mom would push some aside and tell Mrs. Dirian she'd get them at another time.

I am 65 years old at the time of this writing, and I still totally remember that look of despair. That's why I took care of my mom for many years. I am poor no more, so I could do it. She lived to be 90 years old. I paid for pretty much everything. I told her to spend what little money she had on herself and that I would pay all her bills. I know everyone cannot afford to do this, but I could. If you can honor your mom and dad this way, you should do it. Even if you can't do everything, do something to be honorable.

Well, as I grew up, I began to beat this poverty demon. You can too. We do not, and we will not, submit to its ways any longer.

I ended up enlisting in the Marines. I was deployed twice to Vietnam, once for 10 months and once for 11. I only came home to see my Vickie for about 3 weeks in between.

After our second tour, we were told by our captain that we would be stopping at a port on the way back to the States and should buy a gift for our mom or sweetheart and anyone close to us. I immediately thought of Vickie and my mom. I loved my grandma, but she passed away while I was in Vietnam. The only other person I really thought about was Mrs. Dirian. So I bought her a gift too.

Once home, my family had a reunion for me. I pulled away to go see Mrs. Dirian. When I arrived at the little corner store, there was an older couple exiting the store. I asked them if Mrs. Dirian was still alive, and they confirmed that she was and was actually inside.

I ran into the store like I did as a kid. I went to the end of her counter where the four Barclay boys used to line up, and I stood there, just like I did years ago, only this time I was in Marine Corps dress blues with all my medals. As she looked at me, she came over to those saloon doors. (Funny how they had shrunk over the years.) She looked at me and looked at me and finally realized who I was. "Bibs?" she asked. "Yes, ma'am," I answered. She said, "Son, that won't work anymore!" We laughed.

When I explained what the captain said and how I thought about who was important to me and that she was on that list with only my mom and my wife, she began to cry. She asked me why I would do this. I told her that as a little kid, I watched from behind her counter, staring into my mother's face and noticing her countenance as she couldn't pay for enough food for us—that gray look, that face of fear and despair. I told her that I remember how she always added food back into our box or bag as we went to the car and how when we got home, Mom would empty out those groceries and see the extras, and her whole face would change. I told her how she brought a little hope to my mom. I said, "And furthermore I don't believe you ever charged my mom for any of that candy." It was a great moment for both of us.

I finally beat "little bit." Just like the widow woman in Elisha's life, I know I will have to contend with it and the other demons of mammon the rest of my life, as we all must, but I know how to beat it now.

I actually look forward to meeting this widow woman in Heaven. She changed my life forever. I have since learned to obey the prophet at all costs. Vickie and I have given our way out of poverty. We learned that you don't reap what you *want;* you reap what you *sow.* Every phase of our life we have had "little bit" whisper in our ear saying, "Who do you think you are?" or "You are not good enough to do this." Each and every time I take my thumb and finger and flip it off my shoulder and go on to obey my God.

It feels so good to know that I will never be bound by these five demons again because I learned how to spiritually deal with them and bind them. I want to encourage you today that God made a way for you to whip mammon for the rest of your life. No, not once and for all, but every time it comes around to mess with you.

5

UGLY CHILDHOOD, UGLY CHILD

I hated my childhood. No, I wasn't abused by either parent—not physically, not sexually, and not verbally. I was abused by demons that made our life tough and hurt my mama very badly. I felt (what was intended to be) a lifelong ripping in my soul as I watched my dad pretty much shrivel up and die on the couch. I hated watching all my friends grow up with a dad when I didn't have one. In fact, I might have hated them for it. I hated living as a prisoner to poverty. I hated standing in welfare food lines for food, rain or shine. I hated the food, and I guess I hated the people who handed it out.

I'm not really sure why I had such a bad temper and would go almost blind throwing tantrums. After I hurt someone or destroyed something, I would "come to" and not even remember much of it. I remember getting so angry that I would go after anyone, no matter how big or how much older than me. I had few friends in school because of my rage. I beat up most of them at one time or another. I stabbed my younger brother in the rear with a three-pronged pitchfork. I don't remember why I did it, but I remember him running, yelling to Mom, and screaming for help with the pitchfork handle trailing him and the fork in his rump.

I remember chasing my older brother with a steel poker from the wood stove. I was going to hurt him bad. Thank God he could outrun me (barely).

One time I got so mad I stoned my grandma through the front picture window of our house. I hated being like this, but there was no help for me. My fuse was so short that it took very little to set me off.

Once a boy at school talked trash about my mom. When I heard it, I hunted him down. I remember slugging him in the face and knocking him out. Every time I saw him I would want to do it again. All the kids at school passed the word to "stay away from Barclay; he has issues." I hated this. I hated being this way.

I met Vickie going into the seventh grade. We were barely 13. I fell in love with her the moment I saw her. Seriously! I haven't stopped chasing her to this day. Once the word was out that I was interested in her, she was "off limits." Even the seniors wouldn't talk to her because they knew I was crazy and would go after them. Vickie hated this. She basically had only girls and relatives for friends.

I was banned from school in the eleventh grade because of my aggression. Before that I was escorted to school by the truant officer almost every day. I didn't really miss school, but I missed being with Vickie every day. I actually didn't see any need for school until I was in the Marines and ended up attending the Army and Navy Academy for my diploma. I think I was the oldest guy in the class.

I'm not sure why I had such a bad temper and such a short fuse. I can only tell you I did, and I could not get rid of it.

DAD'S DEAD

I remember the day I was denied the access to go and see my dad. He was in the hospital in Mount Pleasant, Michigan. He was dying. We went to the hospital as a family. We gathered in the lobby waiting area. One or two at a time, people were going up to see him. My turn never came. I wasn't old enough, I was told. I was denied access. My father died in that hospital room, and my two younger brothers and I were not allowed to say goodbye. I guess they had rules. Stupid rules. If I could have found who made up those rules I would have influenced them to change them. I suppose they thought a young man my age couldn't handle seeing my dad on his deathbed with all the tubes and machines, but all it did for me (being denied entry) was drive the anger in deeper.

THE FUNERAL

I don't remember everything about my dad's funeral, but I do remember standing at the side of the open casket, and the preacher had his hand on me. I was staring at my dad's body. It was cold. He was gone. It was too late to say goodbye.

I clearly remember the preacher saying to me that God needed my dad in Heaven and that is why He took him from me. When I heard that, my blood curdled within me. I felt a rage go inside of me. I kicked the preacher in the shins and yelled at him, "You are a liar!" I'm not sure why I said that. I just couldn't accept that excuse. I hated those words. I hated everything. I hated everyone.

I ran home from the funeral home. Anger and rage consumed me. I began to throw the tantrum of all tantrums. I remember yelling at the top of my lungs. My bedroom was upstairs. I took the pieces of furniture one at a time and literally threw them down the stairs until my room was pretty much empty. I never wanted to see anyone ever again.

I got over that day, but things were never the same. I had issues. Severe anger issues grew greater. I copped an attitude and was driven by it. I fought everything and everybody. I only remember being kind to my mom and Vickie Lynn St. Dennis. I was pretty much at war with everyone else.

I became a childhood alcoholic. That's right. Alcohol had controlled me and abused me ever since I was young. You abuse alcohol at first, and then it will pay you back. In the end it will abuse *you*. One might think this is impossible, a child getting enough booze to become an alcoholic. Where would a child get booze? But when you belong to a family that drinks, it is available everywhere. It was in the cabinets, left in glasses on the table, in the fridge, in cars, and about everywhere else.

I was sick. I was hung over most mornings. This only added trauma to my already dark days. I hated this, but there was no way out for me. I remember sitting in our family doctor's office when Dr. Wilson told my mom that he thought I was bleeding inside and that she must get me off alcohol or I would never see 18, 19, or 20 years old. I wasn't quite a teenager yet.

I will testify later how the Lord and His church got me free from alcohol, nicotine, profanity, rage, inner anger, insecurity, fear, and tantrums. He whom the Son sets free is free indeed!

VIETNAM WAR—I'M GOING!

When I was 18, I was no better. I fell asleep every night, scared and feeling evil all around me. I hated that. I felt hopeless. I felt so empty. I felt so alone. Something was driving me. I felt like hurting everyone. I wanted to lash out at the whole world. When I realized I could do this legally, I joined the Marines and volunteered for Vietnam.

On the last night of Marine Corps boot camp we sat around with our DI (drill instructor), and he treated us halfway decent for the first time since we met him. He read off our MOS (military occupation, job assignment) to each one of us. When he read my name, he added, "You got your way, Barclay. You're shipping to Vietnam. And by the way, what has made you so mean?"

I shipped twice—once for 11 months, and once for 10. It was there during my second deployment that I really met Jesus Christ and was totally and truly born again. I was a new creation. Well, at least on the inside. (More on this later.)

It's weird how you bring your childhood with you wherever you go. That's why we have to make sure our churches are strong, and our children's church workers and teachers are highly anointed. You only pass through childhood once in your lifetime. If you're young and you are struggling like I was, there is a way out. There truly *is*. His name is Jesus!

6

I MET JESUS

As a young man, I had only heard about Jesus Christ. I remember the Oral Roberts show on our black-and-white TV. A few years ago the Rev. Mark Barclay had the opportunity to thank Dr. Roberts for his impact on my life. At lunch one day I told Brother Roberts that he was my discipline as a child. My mom would say, "If you boys do bad this week, you'll sit and watch the Oral Roberts show on Sunday!" I'm not sure why my mom did this because she wasn't religious at all. When I told Dr. Roberts this, he said to me, "Well, Mark, I guess it didn't do you too bad, did it?"

I remember getting caught stealing a candy bar at the local grocery store by the man who stocked the shelves. He was a Christian, and he lectured us pretty good and told us about Jesus Christ. We reluctantly gave back the candy bars but totally ignored the lecture.

I remember three young people coming to my apartment door in Carlsbad, California. This was just after I came back from my first deployment to Vietnam. I hardly remember anything they said or the literature they tried to pass off to me. I do remember running them off and threatening their life. Even after I physically chased them off, one of them came back the next day. As I ran him off again, he yelled at me as he ran across the parking lot, "You better get your life right with God because He has a call on you."

This wouldn't escape me. It sort of haunted me. It was always on my mind. I kept wondering about this young man who came back to witness to me again the next day. Why would he do that? Why would he risk my hurting him again and running him off again? I just couldn't get his words out of my head.

Then the day came when I decided to ask the Lord to come into my heart. Everything in me exploded. It was the first time I really felt alive inside. I truly had a special, personal encounter with Jesus Christ. I truly was born again.

Nothing on the outside changed at all. I still drank, cussed, smoked, chewed, and fought, but it wasn't the same. On the inside there was no more hatred. There was no more deep sorrow or insecurity. I felt alive and strong. I felt so clean. I didn't want to hurt anyone ever again. On the contrary, I wanted to help people with all my heart.

2 CORINTHIANS 5:17

Therefore if any man *be* in Christ, *he is* a new creature: old things are passed away; behold, all things are become new.

This defined me so well. I was a new creature inside for sure. There was no doubt in my mind. I knew it immediately. I judge no man's confession or claimed conversion, but I do doubt how some of them can confess Christ and not chase Him. Everything in me demanded that I chase Him. It wasn't just a prayer. It wasn't just a decision. It was a true conversion. I knew I would explode inside if I didn't learn more about Him.

I also noticed that I was no longer full of hatred. I immediately lost my reason for hurting people. I just didn't feel that driving force anymore. Thank You, Jesus!

I came out of Vietnam a Christian—not a disciple, by any means, but surely a Christian. I knew my days of fighting humans were over, and my fight now was to find this Jesus and His people and know Him and find out what He wanted from me.

I soon learned that I was in a new war—a war just as deadly and as crucial as Vietnam. It was a war against my flesh. It was a battle to kick the devil and his demons out of my life.

The war was on, and as any good Marine would say, I will not surrender. I do not negotiate with terrorists, and I take no prisoners. I will improvise, adapt, and overcome! I will be courageous. Semper Fi—do or die!

7

THE WAR IS ON!

I was about 22 years old and had 2 years of Vietnam under my belt. I was a weapons expert, a natural warrior. Win at all costs, or die trying. Fight with air support, artillery, grenades, and your rifle. Shoot that rifle until you run out of bullets, then use your pistol. Shoot that pistol until you run out of bullets, then "fix bayonets." When you can't thrust anymore, then club with the rifle butt. When you can't do that anymore, break out the Ka-Bar. Then it's time for hand-to-hand combat.

However, I soon learned that you cannot shoot or stab a demon. Among the first things the church taught me was that we are in a spiritual warfare and that our enemies are invisible and supernatural, and no natural weapon would defeat them.

EPHESIANS 6:12

For we wrestle not against flesh and blood, but against principalities, against powers, against the rulers of the darkness of this world, against spiritual wickedness in high *places*.

2 CORINTHIANS 10:4-5

…(for the weapons of our warfare *are* not carnal, but mighty through God to the pulling down of strong holds;) casting down imaginations, and every high thing that exalteth itself against the knowledge of God, and bringing into captivity every thought to the obedience of Christ…

1 PETER 5:8-9

Be sober, be vigilant; because your adversary the devil, as a roaring lion, walketh about, seeking whom he may devour: whom resist stedfast in the faith, knowing that the same afflictions are accomplished in your brethren that are in the world.

I am so grateful that the church people and my first pastor helped me learn these things. For me, they didn't come easily. I don't know if I was just a slow learner, or if it was just so absolutely opposite from how I had lived my life up until that time. Perhaps satan had blinded my mind so that the light of the glorious gospel would not shine on me.

2 CORINTHIANS 4:4

…in whom the god of this world hath blinded the minds of them which believe not, lest the light of the glorious gospel of Christ, who is the image of God, should shine unto them.

For the first time ever I felt that maybe I could be free from all these habits and practices that were ruining my life. I felt a glimmer of hope on the inside. I still had habits and I hated them, but my heart was clean; and though I knew little about God and His Word, I somehow knew that He knew that I wanted to be free. So here I was, for the first time in my life, searching how to break the bands of wickedness and better my life in Christ. My goal was to not just be a Christian inside but become a disciple, a believer who could actually live the life of Christ.

I declared war on my flesh and began to attack it with great prejudice. So how does one do this? How do you fight spiritual warfare? How do you fight and defeat an invisible enemy? If natural weapons don't work (and they don't), what are my new weapons, and how do I use them? Better question yet, how do I find out? Who will train me?

I went into the Marines knowing no other Marine and knowing nothing about them. I didn't even get to watch a training video. It was raw Marine Corps shock treatment upon arrival. I felt the same way now entering this new Kingdom called the kingdom of God. I really never knew a Christian and knew nothing about living as one.

All the rules had changed. The warfare had changed. The enemy had changed. The weapons had changed. The lifestyle had changed. The environment had changed. Even the vocabulary had changed.

I knew I needed a spiritual DI to teach me and instruct me. I set out to find a church. I remembered back, sitting in a bar in Subic Bay in the Philippines. The Lord instructed me to look around the room. I did, and He said, "Do you want to be like these men and women with whom you drink?" I answered, "No, Sir, not anymore." He said to me, "You must leave them, or you will never be free. You must no longer run with them, but go find My people, and live your new life with them." I could still pick out the well-used barstool where I sat but have never sat upon again since that day!

I set out to find God's people. These were to be *my* people. I set out on a recon mission to find a spiritual DI, an instructor who could teach me how to live this new lifestyle in this new Kingdom.

8

OH, MY GOD—
I'M IN CHURCH!

It was a warm, sunny Carlsbad, California, Sunday morning when I yelled to Vickie, "Get a dress on, Baby—we're going to church!" "Yeah, right," she answered.

When she came into the bedroom and saw that I had dressed up a little, she was blown away. Sometimes I think she still is to this day. I informed her that we were running a recon mission to find a church that would teach us how to better our lives and get out of the flesh pit we had been living in.

Remember, I met her when we were 13 years old, and she happened to know that I had never really been to church before. Well, actually I had been. I had attended vacation Bible school as a young child. It was in a small neighborhood church. I lasted but one day. On the first day the teacher informed us that we would be doing some sports, crafts, Bible study, and so on. When it came to the crafts, she said we were going to build Noah's ark. I never met a Noah and did not know who or what he was, but when she explained that an ark was a massive boat, I was in. She explained to us how we were going to glue Popsicle sticks together to make this ark. Cool, I thought. So on the first day we started our ship-building project.

On the second day, when it came time for crafts, I raised my hand. For a minute or two the teacher ignored me. But I was persistent. Finally she asked me what I wanted. Bad mistake! I said, "Listen, lady, I think I can speak for all us kids here that we are tired of dry sticks. Tomorrow we want sticks with Popsicles still on them. It isn't right that you get to eat them all, and all we get is to glue the sticks. So… no Popsicles, no stupid boat."

Ouch! I got dismissed and taken home. I didn't return. I also got the spanking of my life when my dad found out.

The second time I ever remember attending a church was for our wedding. (Oh, Vickie's mama would send us to the church; but we would just go in, get the bulletin, and leave.) Vickie and I got married in a small Baptist church in Harrison, Michigan. Believe me, it was for picture-taking purposes only. I still remember what the preacher asked us when we met for the pre-marriage discussion. "Son," he said, "Do you know Jesus as your Savior?" "No," I said. "Well, do you want to?" "No," I answered. He then turned to Vickie and asked her the same question. She pointed to me and said, "Well, if *he* does." I have always told Vickie that was the dumbest answer she ever gave in her whole life.

Vickie's mama (Shirley) hated me. Looking back, I can't blame her. I was such a mess as a teenager. Any mom in her right mind would not want her daughter dating me or anyone as messed up as me. Back then, I just hated her back.

She demanded that if I wanted to date Vickie, I had to go to church with her on Sunday. At that time Shirley was a backslidden Baptist and didn't go to church herself. I never agreed to go, but Vickie volunteered me. Believe me, even though Vickie was a much better person than me, she had no intention of going to church either. So I wondered why she was committing me. We would drive by the Baptist church and pick up a bulletin in the entryway and then go do our thing. When I dropped Vickie off at home, we were questioned by Mama Shirley about whether we went to church or not. Of course we did (long enough to grab a bulletin). After a while Mama Shirley got wise to this and began to ask who was there in attendance, so we would stop by the church and pick up our bulletin and look through the glass entry doors to find a name or two to tell her.

And that, my friend, is my churchgoing experience growing up. So when I said to Vickie, "Get a dress on, Baby—we're going to church!" she was blown away.

I clearly remember this day, and I actually remember the church. As we were driving to it, Vickie asked me how I would know if it was what I was looking for, because we had never been to church. I said, "I don't know, Vickie. I have no idea what we are looking for, but I want to find God's people and be like them. So let's recon this joint and see what it's like." As we got to the parking lot, she asked me again. My answer: "Vickie, you and I know nothing about church, but we do know this—if they act like me, cuss like me, and drink like me, then we are out of here because we already have plenty of friends like that."

I know this, if I would have walked into a church like some of today's churches and heard the pastor cuss from the pulpit, the deacons talk about their beer, and they were all dressed like they were going to a beach party, I would probably still be bound to this day.

That church was wonderful, though it wasn't where we settled. We ended up attending a smaller church in Escondido, just outside the back gate of Camp Pendleton where I was stationed. There I met the church that removed my graveclothes and found the pastor (the spiritual DI) who would end up making a great disciple out of me.

I felt clean in church. Every service made me feel alive and cleansed. I was so dirty and so bound. I would just sit in church and bow my head and thank God I was there and that I felt so good being there. I spent many hours at the altars. I responded to every altar call that fit me or even came close to fitting me. There was just something about surrendering my life to Christ and His Word.

I remember the first time I ever heard a message in tongues, a gift of the Spirit (1 Cor. 12:7-9). Our worship service had just ended, and the congregation was singing in the spirit in their heavenly language. It suddenly became silent in the sanctuary. Then a person blurted out loud with this speaking in tongues. I thought, oh my God, what is *that?* Then another person with a loud voice declared they had the interpretation to that tongue (another gift of the Spirit). They shouted out, "Thus saith the Lord… " I remember turning to Vickie and saying, "Who did he say was going to talk?" Vickie grabbed my hand and told me to hush. I did not realize how loud I was when I spoke to her, but it silenced the man giving the message in tongues (and the rest of the church). There was a dead-quiet pause, and then the man said again that God was going to speak. And He did. Wow! I never heard or felt anything like it at any time in my life.

When I got home that day after church, I sat on the edge of my bed with my Bible. Vickie came in and sat next to me and asked if I was okay and what I thought of the church service. I said it was a little weird, and I had never seen or heard anything like it in my life. She asked if that meant we weren't going back. I answered, "Oh no, we'll be going back. Something happened to me in that church service."

Some people say that speaking in tongues and any display of the Holy Spirit is offensive and runs off visitors. Not so. It is a sign to them who believe not. God said so. No man is smarter than God. I am a witness to the effect that the demonstration of God has on one's life.

As a sinner, I had an extremely foul mouth. But when you are a sinner, you don't realize it. At least I never did. I remember the pastor teaching a class on casting out demons and binding the devil. He did a special set of church services on spiritual warfare. At the end of one of the sessions he had us all stand in a circle, maybe five to seven people per circle.

Vickie and I were in one of those circles. We each were to take a turn at binding the devil.

The first person in our circle began, and we continued to go around the circle. When it got to the person closest to me, I began to think, I can do this. This is no problem for a United States Marine. My turn finally came. With a loud voice I began to bind the devil. "Devil," I said. "I bind you in the name of Jesus, you [blankety-blankety-blank] devil." The other believers quickly released my hand, including Vickie. It got completely quiet in that church. I realized what I had done. I looked up and saw the pastor coming directly toward me. I also saw a dear old saint we called "Sister Pentecost" coming toward me. She had prayed for me sometimes. I decided to go with the pastor rather than her, but before I could get to him she came flying through the air, jumped on me, grabbed ahold of both of my ears and part of my hair, and began to cast out some demon.

The pastor was extremely clear, and I saw the fire in his eyes. "Get to my office," he said. "Now!" I knew I was doomed. He commanded me to never speak again until he gave me permission. Though I knew he meant it, it wasn't quite as severe as Sister Pentecost. She said if I were to ever speak like that again, God would judge me and I could drop dead. I believed her. And it was the beginning of my deliverance from such a deadly, poisonous tongue.

I went to work the next day with recruits. I was still a Marine instructor at this time. I yelled for the recruits to fall in. They did so with typical boot camp energy. As I began to speak to one recruit, I said, "Private, you… Private, you…" Scared half to death because of what Sister Pentecost said, I found myself not knowing how to even do my job! I called the pastor at noon (pre-cell phone days) and told him that I thought he had ruined my career and that I was now mute. What is an instructor to say to a recruit? "Come on, sweetie, you can do it," or "Come on, darling, I know you can do one more sit-up, can't you, honey child?" I DON'T THINK SO!

What a blessing to belong to a church that can set you free from the things that are hurting your life and stopping you from advancing in life. It wasn't long, and I was totally free. No more corrupt communication was coming out of my mouth—not even when I was angry. I praise God for this!

One day after church I remember a couple inviting us out. This was really big to us. When you're new to a church and you already feel that you're not good enough to fit in, it means everything to be invited to fellowship. We went to a nearby restaurant with a handful of church members. It all started out great, but after we had ordered our meal, one of them began to verbalize his disagreement with the pastor. In fact, once he started, a couple others jumped in. The conversation turned not only negative but almost slanderous. I told Vickie we were leaving. When the other believers asked me what was wrong and why was I leaving, I quickly informed them that I had been misunderstood. "You have made a grave mistake," I said. "I am not like this. I am so disappointed in all of you. I was so thrilled to be invited to this after-church fellowship, but now I'm ashamed to sit at this table with you. Shame on each of you for saying amen so vigorously toward Pastor's message and then sitting here with no shame and not only disagree but do it to his discredit. If this is called fellowship, count me out."

That word spread very rapidly through the church, and for the longest time no one would invite Vickie and me to their home or to go out for fellowship. As much as I wanted to belong, I refused to be around this behavior or have my clean feeling about the church dirtied like this. It was a great relief to me when different ones who were at that table slowly came to me privately and apologized for their words and their behavior. Though I never got close to any of them, I think maybe they all began to enjoy our church and our pastors even more.

One day after church, as we were leaving the sanctuary, a handful of us brothers were standing at the front steps. The pastor came out and said something to one of the brothers. That brother just totally rebuked our pastor to his face. The next thing I remember was the brothers pulling me off from him and saying, "Don't hit him again, Mark." I guess I went after him in the finest Marine Corps fashion. I punched him in the face and took him down and was going to punch him again. When I realized what I was doing, I was so ashamed. I felt so small. I went to my car and headed for my house, certain I would never return to the church again. And I actually meant it. I already felt so small around those great church people. How could I face them after what I had just done?

I remember that same brother calling me on the phone that afternoon. He told me he was coming over to bring me to church that evening. I told him that was not going to happen and hung up the phone. He called back a few minutes later and said, "I will come and get you; you're going back to church with me." I told him I was not going, that I did him bad, I embarrassed Pastor, I embarrassed my wife, and I have proven that I cannot fit into the church environment. Then I hung up the phone. About an hour before church my doorbell rang, and it was that brother. He said, "Mark, I forgive you. I was wrong to speak that way toward Pastor, and I have repented to him. I probably deserved to be punched like that. But you can't do that again, not to me or anyone else. Do you understand?"

We got to church late. The song service was already in full swing. Wouldn't you know it, he reserved two seats almost to the front row. As I came in from the back of the church and worked my way to our seats and passed each row of believers, they began to clap. I could read some lips as they were saying things like welcome back, or thank you for not leaving us, or we forgive you. By the time I got to my seat, the song service had stopped, and the whole church was clapping. Pastor was in the pulpit. He shook his long finger at me and said, "No more of that, and welcome back, son."

That was the beginning of my deliverance from violence, uncontrolled anger, and being a striker. I will say it time and again: To be delivered from anger and violence and to have self-control and no more temper tantrums is a wonderful gift from God. Since my water baptismal service, God is my witness, I have never once lost my temper all these decades later.

One day Pastor called me into his office and had me take a seat. He pointed at the door and said, "See that door?" "Yes, sir," I answered. "Well, I do not have time to invest in you if you are going to flake out on me. There are too many other people who want my time. I am an expert disciple maker. I can make a disciple out of you, Mark, but only if you are serious. If not, head out that door." "No, sir," I replied, "I am in for the long haul." He was right on, and so was I. Here I am, decades later, still serving the Lord. I have never turned back.

Don't treat me like I'm breakable! This is what I told my first pastor. I asked to speak with him one day after church. He agreed. I said, "Pastor, I noticed you treat people like they are fragile and very breakable. I don't mean to insinuate that I know anything about pastoring. I certainly do not. In fact, I barely know how to be a Christian yet. I just noticed these things, and I ask you not to treat me like that. I am way behind these others. I want to know the Word of God and how to be a great disciple. You cannot offend me. I give you my word on it. Just look me in the face and tell me the blunt truth. Then I will work on it until I conquer it."

Believe me, he obliged! But I was never offended at the things he pointed out in my life. I learned later this was part of his duty as a pastor.

2 TIMOTHY 4:2 AMPC

Herald *and* preach the Word! Keep your sense of urgency [stand by, be at hand and ready], whether the opportunity seems to be favorable or unfavorable. [Whether it is convenient or inconvenient, whether it is welcome or unwelcome, you as preacher of the Word are to show people in what way their lives are wrong.] And convince them, rebuking *and* correcting, warning *and* urging *and* encouraging them, being unflagging *and* inexhaustible in patience and teaching.

Nothing Pastor pointed out to me offended me or discouraged me. It gave me things to work on and things to lay on the altar before God. I am thankful to this day. Everything he pointed out to me, I attacked, and God delivered me from each of them. (More on this in the coming chapters.)

I was so hungry to know more of God. I couldn't stay away from the church services. I sometimes would go and sit in the church parking lot, even though no one was around. I fell in love with the Word of God immediately. I couldn't get enough of it. It was changing my life forever. Light was coming in where only darkness once existed.

I went to absolutely every church service, every men's meeting, every work party, every prayer meeting, every class. I would even volunteer to serve at the board meetings and the deacons' meetings (though I didn't belong to either team), just so I could get more information and learn more about how the Kingdom operated. Our church had a program for boys called Royal Rangers. The Royal Rangers loved it when I came to their meeting wearing my Marine Corps uniform. I was definitely the hero of that group. Many times I was busy teaching them about outdoor things.

During Royal Rangers I learned there was another program for the girls called Missionettes. I may actually be the only male preacher ever to get a certificate for completing the Missionettes program! Our church was in California, so most of the time the Royal Rangers and the Missionettes met in the backyard of our properties. Our church had a stairway that went to another room, which was normally used as a classroom. I was so hungry to learn the Bible that I would sneak into that upper room and wait for the teacher to come and teach the Bible to the Missionettes.

Nobody but God ever knew I was there until one day I got so caught up in the teacher's message that I yelled, "Amen." The moment I did it, I knew I was doomed. I could hear that woman coming up the steps. When she got to the upper room and opened the door, there I was. Caught! Busted!

She immediately began to interrogate me. "What on earth are you doing here?" she asked. I said, "Ma'am, I learn so much from listening to your simple teachings to these girls that I just can't stay away. I feel desperate to learn the Bible to become a better Christian." She said she planned to tell Pastor about this. I pleaded with her not to and that no harm was done and that the girls never even knew I was there. She did not seem to be striking a bargain with me at all and told me to hide until after class and never come back. I did not keep my end of the bargain, and I certainly went back and continued to learn the Bible from this dear woman.

On the Sunday morning of the Missionettes' graduation, I witnessed those same girls graduate from their program. And at the end of the program I discovered that she never did tell Pastor about catching me in the upper room. How, you ask? When all the certificates were handed out, she looked at Pastor and said there is one more that we must present today to someone who never missed a class. Then she called out my name and called me to the front of the church. She told the story and presented me with a certificate of completion. The church laughed (though Pastor didn't seem to). But I didn't care because I had learned so much about the Bible and about Jesus Christ from that dear lady teacher.

9

LOOSE HIM, AND LET HIM GO FREE

I am writing this book, which is a form of my autobiography and especially my testimony, because I was raised a sinner, but now I am a God-possessed being.

I tell many people that I maximized "sinship," so I now work at maximizing sonship. I was in so much personal internal struggle and trouble as a young man that I would go to bed every night feeling evil in me and evil all around me. Every night I would lie on my bed and think about how ashamed of me my mama was because of my behavior. I was already so bound. As I mentioned in the previous chapter, after my father died, evil tried to possess me. I was mad at the world, at everything and everyone. But alone in the dark of the night by myself I would lie in my bed and wonder why I wanted to hurt people so badly, and I worried about my future.

Maybe your upbringing or background is as worldly and radical as mine, maybe not. I believe with all my heart that I was delivered so I could be a voice and vessel of deliverance for many other people. I just didn't know about any of this at the time. But once I invited the Lord into my heart, everything changed. I mean, everything on the inside. No more demons for me. No more darkness. If you're still bound or driven, this can be your story as well.

The devil will try anything to stop us from serving God. He absolutely hates to let anybody go. Even after I was born again for a season and serving God, the devil would still come to me and tell me that he would stop me and even kill me early. My life is a chain of healing and delivering miracles for me, my family, and those to whom the Lord has sent me. We know them as miracles. But the devil meant them for harm and evil. My life is a living witness of a believer who has signs following him (Mark 16:17).

I recall having a horrible demonic visitation one night. I had been born again for a few months. I woke in the middle of the night, gasping for air. The devil was shouting at me that he would kill me. I had just been attacked in the spirit realm by two vicious attack dogs, Doberman Pinschers, biting at my throat. With everything within me I was trying to yell, "In the name of Jesus…" but I couldn't get it out. One would attack, and then the other. It was so real I knew it was more than just a dream. The spirit of death was in my room. I finally sat up in the bed, and from the top of my lungs the name of Jesus finally came out of my mouth. I ran to the door (a sliding door from our bedroom into the yard) and slid it open, and I commanded these demons to get out of my life, once and for all. They have never been back. I confirmed that day that the name of Jesus is above every other name, including the spirit of death.

Read these verses out loud:

JOHN 11:41

Then they took away the stone *from the place* where the dead was laid. And Jesus lifted up *his* eyes, and said, Father, I thank thee that thou hast heard me.

JOHN 11:42

And I knew that thou hearest me always: but because of the people which stand by I said *it*, that they may believe that thou hast sent me.

JOHN 11:43

And when he thus had spoken, he cried with a loud voice, Lazarus, come forth.

JOHN 11:44

And he that was dead came forth, bound hand and foot with grave clothes: and his face was bound about with a napkin. Jesus saith unto them, Loose him, and let him go.

This may be one of the most powerful sets of verses in all the gospels. It certainly is to me. I believe with all my heart this is the duty of the New Testament Church. Simply said, Lazarus was called out of the tomb of death to resurrection life. But he came forth bound, hand and foot. Jesus told His disciples to loose him from his graveclothes and let him go free.

This is exactly the work of the New Testament Church. Jesus calls us out of the old life. He calls us out of the tomb that encapsulated us (the world, the things of this world, and a soul that was headed for eternal damnation). But just because we accept Christ and are born again doesn't mean we're fixed yet. We are truly born of the Spirit of God. We are truly Christians. But there are many things that must be taken away from us. We need deliverance and separation from our habits and that old fallen and cursed nature and its behavior.

This is my story. I actually met Jesus Christ. There's no doubt about it. The conversion in my heart was explosive. There is no other way to explain it. My head did not accept knowledge. My heart was totally converted, and I was regenerated. "Therefore if any man *be* in Christ, *he is* a new creature: old things are passed away; behold, all things are become new" (2 Cor. 5:17).

MY WATER-BAPTISM EXPERIENCE

This is on the top of my list as one of the greatest events in my life. I was first taught from the Scriptures (mainly Romans 6) about the mighty supernatural power of water baptism.

Our pastor was teaching on what happens to you physically and supernaturally when you are water-baptized. I was so moved by his teaching that I was driven to have this done in my life as quickly as possible. As I sat there, he began to explain the spiritual ramifications and the mighty delivering power that aids Christians in getting their flesh under control. I knew for sure this would be my day of deliverance. A date was scheduled. I could hardly wait and kept working on our pastor to move it up.

I was working for the Marines at a rifle range at Camp Pendleton as a marksmanship instructor. I was consumed with the thought that I would finally be free—free from all the bondages and sins that were ruining my life. I went to the base that day and stood outside the barracks and yelled, "Fall in!" Immediately the tarmac was filled with lean, mean, fighting machines called U.S. Marines. When they had assembled, I yelled another command: "Aah-tench-hut." I had their undivided attention. I remember telling them that their sergeant was being water-baptized for the remission of sins on this certain day, and I knew they would enjoy being in attendance (in fact, woe to the man who missed this great occasion).

Finally baptism day came. The room was filled with Marines, family, and friends. What a day it was! When my pastor submerged me, he did what he always threatened to do and held me down longer. When I came out of that water face first, I felt evil leave me. It's actually the first time in my life I remember not feeling evil or angry. Anger left me that day. Many years have now gone by, and I haven't lost my temper since that day in the baptismal tank. Oh sure, I get angry, but I never lose my temper. It was like I had instant self-control. I was and still am so excited about this because I hurt so many things and so many people when that rage was driving me and that pent-up anger was released. Thank God for His deliverance. From the day of my baptism I continued to be delivered from all hindering forces until one day I was totally free. Over 40 years have gone by, and I am still free to this day.

If you fight rage, have fits of rage, lose your temper, or throw tantrums, there is hope for you. First of all, be sure you are in a church family that recognizes you have this gravecloth still on you and that it is their duty to do their part to help get you free. If you are in a church that doesn't even believe this way, you may be doomed and a slave to your bondage all your life.

Second, don't ever let discouragement win. Even though you have tried all you know to do to be free, keep laying it on the altar of God and declaring with your mouth that you are free. You will reap if you don't faint. "And let us not be weary in well doing: for in due season we shall reap, if we faint not" (Gal. 6:9).

PRAISE GOD, I GOT FILLED WITH THE HOLY GHOST!

ACTS 1:8

But ye shall receive power, after that the Holy Ghost is come upon you: and ye shall be witnesses unto me both in Jerusalem, and in all Judaea, and in Samaria, and unto the uttermost part of the earth.

ACTS 2:39

For the promise is unto you, and to your children, and to all that are afar off, *even* as many as the Lord our God shall call.

Our pastor kept saying that we need this power from on high. Sometimes he referred to it as the infilling of the Holy Spirit or the baptism in the Holy Spirit. All I knew was that I needed this power.

One day in our church an altar call was given for those who wanted to be filled with the Holy Ghost. I think I may have been the first one to race to that altar as they laid hands on the believers. Just like in the Book of Acts when they began to speak with a heavenly language, as they got to me, I felt them lay their hands on me but only after I felt a surge of God's power. It sort of overwhelmed me and almost overpowered me. I thought for sure I was going to hit the ground. It first got upon me and began to quicken my body, and then it went deep inside me. It's hard to put in English, but it seemed at the time like it went so deep inside there was a part of me I had not known existed—my deepest, innermost being.

I spoke a few words of a language I had never spoken before, a heavenly language. I found out later this was proper, biblical, and very supernatural. I knew my life was changed forever. As I left that altar for my seat, I tried everything within me to speak in these "tongues" again, but all that came out were a few syllables. Though I was excited about what happened, I felt a little disappointed about not being able to just let it flow as people around me did.

As the day and evening went by, I became more and more burdened and even bothered that I could not just speak in tongues like other people seemed to be able to do. I tried everything and learned quickly that this is not something that you are able to do or that your mind can produce. Why was this happening to me? My mind even began to convince me that maybe I really was not filled with the Holy Spirit after all.

The next day I was working with U.S. Marine recruits as a marksmanship instructor on the firing line at Edson Range, Camp Pendleton. But my mind was not really on my job; it was on speaking in tongues. I kept asking the Lord to fill (or refill?) me, or to do it in a way that it would take hold this time. In those days I did not understand how all this worked. I just knew I needed that power, and I needed my prayer language. As I walked up and down that firing line, looking at recruits in the prone position while shooting at their targets, I felt that same surge of power that I did at the altar, only this time it wasn't coming *upon* me; it was coming out *from* me. And before I knew it, I had both hands in the air, and I was yelling out in tongues. The river had been released—that river that comes from your innermost being.

I hadn't realized that the line officer had yelled cease-fire. It became quiet on that firing line as far as I could see to my left and right. The only one making any noise was… ME! I was yelling at the top of my voice in a heavenly language. The line officer left his shack and stepped out on the blacktop and was staring at me. He had both of his hands in the air with that gesture that clearly communicated, "What are you doing? Can you stop playing around so we can get on with our training?" Needless to say, he was an *un*happy camper. My mind began to talk to me and try to convince me to shut up and be ashamed. The Holy Spirit spoke to me and said, "Make up your mind right now whether or not you are going to be ashamed of Me." I remember yelling back at the officer, "I'm just speaking in tongues, sir!"

And I have been speaking in tongues ever since. Through the years I have even had the privilege of having all nine gifts of the Spirit manifest through me to help other people. I don't just *believe* that I am the temple of the Holy Ghost—I *am* the temple of the Holy Ghost. I am a God-possessed human!

I truly have known my Jesus as Savior, healer, and Lord. But I knew Him originally as the master deliverer. I guess it is the driving force that has caused me to work night and day, all these years, to show people a way out of sin, bondage, and bad habits and live a much happier and free life. Many people flirt with sin and are not at all convinced that it is the playground of satan. They don't understand that it will eventually invite a spirit of perversion or a spirit of addiction that will literally disassemble their life, take control, and perhaps even go as far as possess them.

DELIVERED FROM NICOTINE

When I was about nine years old, I smoked my first cigarette. I cannot tell you why. I remember lighting it up and inhaling. It burned my eyes, my nose, and my throat. My mind immediately said, "Stop this. You are killing us. Do not do this to us!"

But my fallen nature drove me to this. Eventually I was consumed with a craving for nicotine, and it was in control of my life, though my mind also told me I could quit anytime I really wanted to. I even ended up chewing tobacco and tried every cigar I could get my hands on and even smoked a pipe for a while. By the time I was 13, I was absolutely, completely addicted to nicotine. And I hated every minute of it.

But when I met a true church family and witnessed that they were clean and not smoking and drinking, I discovered that they possessed the power to get the graveclothes off me. I know without a doubt that Jesus commanded them to loose Mark Barclay and let him go free.

It wasn't instant like the way it was when anger and rage left me. It wasn't instant like when hatred left me. It was a *working* of miracles. I couldn't tell you how many times I tried to quit. I wanted it gone in the worst way. One time I took the whole pack of cigarettes and put them by the rear tire of my car, stomped on the gas, and shredded them to tiny little pieces. I declared that I was free and then stopped at the closest corner store and picked up a new pack.

More than once I would put them on the altar and walk away from them, declaring my freedom, and then once again head for a store and buy another pack. I want to encourage you here. Don't ever stop calling out to God for power over these things because eventually you will conquer them if you just don't faint. "And let us not be weary in well doing: for in due season we shall reap, if we faint not" (Gal. 6:9).

I also want to remind you that the church family never condemned me, but they never condoned my self-destructive behavior either. It seems that some of the modern churches are able to help very few people to get free of graveclothes because the people cry "no condemnation" to the degree that the church won't even address the graveclothes.

On one of those trips to the altar where I left the cigarette pack behind, my addiction to nicotine was stripped from me by the power of God. The elders and the believers kept telling me that if I would just stick with them, they would help get me free. Though I doubted them at times, they turned out to be the deliverers whom Jesus sent to help set me free from the old graveclothes of smoking. Praise God!

That was in the 1970s, and I haven't touched nicotine since. I remember what my brain said when I smoked my last cigarette and committed to God that I would rather die than light up another. My brain said the same thing it did when I smoked my first one: "You're killing us here. Stop it. You can't quit—we'll have a nicotine fit!" Not this time. Not ever again.

If you are fighting a battle with nicotine and addiction, whether smoking or chewing it, there is hope for you. First of all, be sure you are in a church family that recognizes you have this gravecloth still on you and that it is their duty to do their part to help get you free. If you are in a church that doesn't even believe this way, you may be doomed and remain a slave to your bondage all your life.

Second, don't ever let discouragement win. Even though you have tried all you know to do to be free, keep laying it on the altar of God and declaring with your mouth that you are free. You will reap if you don't faint. "And let us not be weary in well doing: for in due season we shall reap, if we faint not" (Gal. 6:9).

DELIVERED FROM ALCOHOL

Our family doctor was Dr. Wilson. I always liked him. Just about the time I was becoming a teenager, I was in his office with him when he told my mom there was a possibility I would never see 18, 19, or 20 years old. "Mrs. Barclay," he said, "Mark is bleeding inside from alcohol abuse. You have to get him out of it." My mom tried but was not very successful. I was so driven and so bound by it.

Over the years I have had people question me and even challenge me about this account. They would ask me how such a young man could have such a drinking problem and how could such a young man find booze. I guess they weren't brought up in a drinking family. There were alcoholic drinks everywhere—in the fridge, in glasses left on tables, in the cabinets, in the vehicles, and everywhere else. It was easy to get our hands on it, and most of our relatives had no problem with our drinking it.

As teenagers, there were so many of us crashing cars and either getting hurt or getting killed that my mom, like many parents of the day, agreed to buy booze for us if we would stay at home and off the streets. Many days it was an endless supply until we passed out, vomited, or both.

It's so strange. I'm not sure why we thought it was so cool. We were all sick all the time. We drank ourselves sick. I never liked the taste of it—none of it. I never liked being drunk. I never liked what it turned me into, and I never liked how it always caused me to hurt people and break things. I certainly never liked the way I felt the next day.

I knew that my first church was aware that I drank. Still, they never condemned me, but they never condoned what I was doing either. They would keep challenging me to stop. In many of the modern churches today they believe that we shouldn't bring up anyone's faults or sins because it's just condemning them. If that is the case, there is hardly any hope for deliverance because it is a form of condoning the sin and sinful nature.

Back to my first church… Again, they never condemned me, but they never condoned my drinking either. I couldn't believe the whole church was dry, on the wagon, non-drinkers. Somehow I knew that if anyone in the church drank, they couldn't set me free. Isn't it amazing that I knew this even as a brand new, baby Christian!

I know myself well enough to know that I would still be alcohol-bound today if I had discovered that any one of those steady church members drank. I was not looking for that. I was hoping they were the true Christians I believed them to be.

I told Vickie I was going to find out who drank and who didn't. So I made a list of the church family members and their cars so I could follow them home. You may ask why I would do that. It is because I needed to know if they were going to stop on the way home and buy booze. I needed to know that they weren't drinking at home and pretending at church.

So I ran a recon mission on each of them. After a few of these specialized snooping missions, Vickie told me she would not ride to church with me anymore and would find her own way home. She would not be in the car with me any longer if I was going to follow people. I told her that I was a good Marine and that no one would ever know I was following them. She didn't buy it at all.

I asked every man in that church if they drank. One at a time they would tell me no. Some would share their testimony of how God set them free from it. Everything in me wanted to believe them.

I finally went to Pastor and asked him if he drank. "Mark," he said, "None of us drink alcohol. We are Christians, and we do not submit to or abuse any substance." I asked, "Are you telling me there is no one in this whole church who drinks?" "Well," he answered, "There is one…" He looked right into my eyes, and I knew he was talking about me.

I wanted to be free so badly. I wasn't looking for a drinking partner or friend. I had plenty of them. Deep inside I was hoping that I would find no drinkers. Then I would know that they really could help set me free. I realize that not everyone is looking for this, but I was. It seems that many want Christ *and* alcohol. It's beyond me because I wanted to be free in the worst way.

I prayed and prayed. I went to every altar call. I read and memorized all the Bible verses the church elders had given me. It just didn't seem to be working. One day the elders came to me and taught me how to fast. They gave me the verses on evil spirits and explained that some only come out with fasting and prayer (Matt. 17:21). I thought they were telling me I was demon-possessed, but they assured me otherwise. They taught me that demons can oppress, depress, and drive a person from the outside. Even Christians can be driven by demonic forces or addicted by them. So I started fasting and praying. I used my mouth to bind these spirits so I could be free.

After some time I was at a church service, and Sister Pentecost came up to me. "How are you doing, beating that booze, sonny boy?" she asked. I was hesitant to answer her because we all respected her walk with God so much and never wanted to disappoint the old gal. I told her it wasn't going so well—that I was trying to do everything the elders said, but it just didn't seem to be working. "Well, what did they tell you to do?" she asked. "Multiple things," I answered. I explained to her the process and the program these elders gave me, which included memorizing verses, changing my confession, fasting, praying, spending time at the altar, and making no provision for the flesh. "Wonderful!" she shouted, and then asked what I was fasting. I told her I was fasting my meals (in those days it was pizza and hamburgers). She answered me with a "Huh, is it pizza and hamburgers you want to be delivered from?" "No ma'am," I quickly answered. She stepped a little closer to me and looked me in the eye and said, "All you are is a hungry drunk! You need to *fast* alcohol if you want to *beat* alcohol." That advice was so simple, but it hit me so hard. Wow, why didn't I think of that? I went to the pastor and the elders with this, and they agreed it was absolutely the right thing to do.

I so remember my first booze fast. My pastor told me that if I would fast, he would fast with me. I got off work from the Marine Corps base and went home that day with no beer stop at the corner store. That in itself seemed so weird. I called Pastor and told him I was fasting alcohol that night and did not plan to drink. He committed to stay up all night and pray and fast with me. He even invited me to come to his house, or he would come to mine. He warned me, though, that if he stayed up all night praying and I was drinking, I would personally meet the Cherokee blood in him. (I think he meant it!)

He called me in the morning, just as I was getting around. Here came the big question: "Mark, did you drink last night?" he asked. "No, sir, I did not," I answered. We praised God together. He again assured me that I was going to beat this thing.

"What are you doing now?" he asked. "Well," I reluctantly answered, "I am drinking a Budweiser." I thought for sure he was going to rebuke me and command me to come and see him. Instead, he taught me a life-changing truth that I have passed on to other people who are trying to get free. He said, "Son, by noon the devil will come to condemn you. He will call you a failure and tell you that you are weak and can't be a good Christian. He will try to convince you that you will be bound to alcohol all your life. You reject him and that flood of thoughts and instead say, 'No way, devil. I made it through an entire night, and I will do it again and again until I am totally free from you and alcohol.'"

Pastor committed to me that anytime I wanted to fast again, he would pray with me and stand with me. What a pastor! And that is exactly what I did. I fasted again, and I made it for two nights. Then I ended up drinking again. I called a third fast and went for three days and nights. No booze. Then I ended up drinking some again. Then I called a fast and went dry for one month with no booze. The fast continued. No booze. After about three months I realized there was really no reason to stop the fast. So, I am still on it, living a fasted life (from alcohol) and walking in liberty and freedom. No booze of any kind enters my lips, and I have been totally free since the 1970s when I started this fast, to the glory of God and the beauty of those saints who knew how to get the graveclothes off me!

If you are fighting a battle with alcohol and you want it gone, there is hope for you. First of all, be sure you are in a church family that recognizes you are bound with this gravecloth still on you and that it is their duty to do their part to help get you free. If you are in a church that doesn't even believe this way, you may be doomed and be a slave to your bondage all your life.

Second, don't ever let discouragement win. Even though you have tried all you know to do to be free, keep laying it on the altar of God and declaring with your mouth that you are free. You will reap if you don't faint. "And let us not be weary in well doing: for in due season we shall reap, if we faint not" (Gal. 6:9).

There are other things from which that young Mark Barclay was delivered. I rejoice over every one of them. God has been so good to me, and now He uses me to help set many other people free. I don't have any way to honestly calculate how many people have been saved, water-baptized, filled with the Spirit, healed, and delivered around the world through our ministry. But it has been my great honor and privilege to lay hands on them and stand with them for a life of freedom from all bondages.

MATTHEW 10:7-8

And as ye go, preach, saying, The kingdom of heaven is at hand. Heal the sick, cleanse the lepers, raise the dead, cast out devils: freely ye have received, freely give.

JOHN 11:44

And he that was dead came forth, bound hand and foot with grave clothes: and his face was bound about with a napkin. Jesus saith unto them, Loose him, and let him go.

10

VICKIE LYNN ST. DENNIS

At the time, Mr. Pat Summerall was the number one announcer for Monday Night Football on TV. I remember the day I got a call from him, asking me if he could do a life story on me. At first I said yes, and then the Lord told me to not do it. Pat said, "Well, I want to do something on you, so let me at least do your story as one of my Summerall Success Stories, and we'll put it on CNN. The Lord gave me permission to do this much.

I flew to Pat Summerall Studios in Texas, and we filmed a clip or two as he requested. In the interview, Pat asked me several questions about my upbringing, the poverty, my dad dying when I was a kid, two trips to Vietnam, etc. He then asked me the secret to my success. Without hesitation, I told him I had met two people who changed my life forever. One was my childhood sweetheart, Vickie St. Dennis. The other was my Lord and Savior, Jesus Christ. This seemed to really intrigue him. He wanted to know more about this.

When the interview was almost over, he asked me a final question: "Any piece of strong advice you can tell our audience?" I told him that one of my greatest secrets of success in life is to GO TO CHURCH, AND LET NO ONE RUN YOU OFF. You may wonder if that's really a great secret to success. Yes, it is! Church has done nothing but fix me and teach me the ways of God. I would trade it for nothing, and I would recommend it to every human alive.

As for my Lord and Savior, Jesus Christ… I told Pat that when I was born again in Vietnam, my whole insides changed, and I became a new creature. Jesus means everything to me. I am very bold to tell everyone I know that I am saved and in love with Jesus. I want the whole world to know that I am a Christian and that I am following Him. Without Christ in my life I am not sure I would even still be alive. I am not ashamed of Jesus or the gospel of Jesus Christ or anything He has done for my family and me.

As for Vickie, she is also a great part of my story. They say that behind every great man is a great woman. It was meant to be that a man should cleave to his wife, his woman, and the two become one. That's Vickie and me—for 52 years (5 years dating, and married 47).

I met Vickie when we were just 13 years old. I first saw her at school. Her family had just moved from Detroit to our little rural town of Harrison. I was standing in the hallway by the cafeteria (where the boys hung out each morning before school started), and my entire world changed when she walked off that bus and into that school. This country boy had never seen anything like it! She was wearing go-go boots and a miniskirt. Wow! I ran home and told my mom that I saw this hot girl get off the bus and I wanted her. My mom said, "Sit down here, Mark. We need to have a 'father'-and-son talk." I pursued Vickie from that moment.

She first became my girlfriend and then my fiancée. When I was 16, I wanted to marry her, but my mom said I had to wait until I was 18. Two weeks after my eighteenth birthday I married her. I was so in love with her it was all I could think about. I still am, and it still is.

At 19 I left for Vietnam where I served as a Marine leader for two tours, one for 10 months and one for 11 months. Vickie was tough. She stood with me and prayed for me. She spent months and months without me. There were no cell phones in those days, and we were rarely in a port where we could make an international call. Vickie would watch the Huntley-Brinkley Report, night after night, as they showed news reports from the combat zone, hoping she would get a glimpse of me. I think military wives are some of the strongest, toughest women alive. I salute every one of them.

When Vickie and I had our two children, Dawn and Joshua, she was more than a mother. She is and always has been the strength of our family. I am not a weak man, and I do not neglect my duties as husband and father; but it is Vickie who has provided the glue that has kept us together and moving forward as a family. I admire her for it, and I admire all wives and mothers who live biblically and their anointing and strength for keeping the family together.

We are a family of miracles. I can choose from many to share with you. My grandson, Malakai, received a miracle healing from a potentially fatal case of Stevens-Johnson syndrome; Trish was diagnosed with cancer and is now cancer free; and my granddaughter, Jadyn, drowned in our pool but was raised again. We are living proof that Jesus is alive, and He still does miracles today.

Let me share just one of our stories: In 2008, Vickie was diagnosed with cancer. I was in the room with her when the doctor said to me, "Reverend, this is aggressive, it is invasive, it has already spread, and it kills most women." Vickie spoke right up with great boldness and pronounced to him that we will get a miracle. "You do what you do, Doc, and Jesus will do what He does, and we will be back with a great testimony."

As we sat in the car that day (before we ever left the parking lot), we discussed how to fight this battle. I learned as a trained combat Marine that you must face fear head-on. If you can't beat the fear, you will most likely never beat that enemy.

I asked Vickie what her biggest fear was. Was it dying? Was it living but in constant pain and battle? We talked bluntly about it, and then we spoke to that fear and submitted it to Jesus Christ. As I sat in that car in the doctor's parking lot, listening to Vickie, the Lord spoke to me: "I did not come that day to kill Goliath. I did not need a testimony. Oh, yes, I could have just blinked My eyes or snorted once and eliminated the entire Philistine army. It was My son who needed the testimony. I came that day to empower My son to kill that giant. And that's what I'm going to do for you and Vickie today."

In 32 days, the cancer was dead and gone. We rejoice in the victory over this killer. We are thankful for all the medical people who were there for us. We will boast in the Lord Jesus Christ for His healing miracle. Ever since that day of victory over cancer and death, I have told people that Jesus is a killer—He kills cancer! He also heals our body.

God revealed to us that day that Vickie's body is not hers. It doesn't belong to her. It was bought and paid for at Calvary. It is the Lord's body. Vickie just gets to live in it. Every cell of it was purchased by the spilt blood of Jesus.

Vickie and I are asked all the time about how we beat this horrible enemy. We say that Vickie prayed the prayer of Hezekiah (2 Kings 20:1-6). "Lord, Mark and I are not fake. We are not pretenders. We don't just preach the gospel—we *live* the gospel. Judge us, and may we not be found lacking or wanting. Lord, if we have served You honorably and properly, then let me live and not die. Add years to my life. If not, then I will see You soon in Heaven."

Vickie clung to the God of the tithe. Through the years we have found ourselves calling upon the Almighty God of the tithe many times, claiming our tither's rights. "God, if we have honored You with the tithe (Heb. 7, Matt. 23:23, Gen. 14:20), then keep Your Word and rebuke this devourer called cancer." HE DID! Thirty-two days after hearing, "This cancer is deadly, aggressive, invasive, spreading, and it kills most women," we were told, "THERE IS NO CANCER TO BE FOUND ANYWHERE IN VICKIE'S BODY!"

Some people thought Vickie was in denial about her initial report, but the truth is, she believed from the beginning that God would heal her. She seldom ever wept over this. It was like God had placed her in a "faith and peace bubble," and no one could get her outside of that to worry and fret. What a woman! What a warrior!

Then, during one of Vickie's annual checkups with the oncologist, the Lord just put the icing on the cake when the doctor told her there was no need to schedule another appointment with him. Her overall health and test results had been so consistently excellent since the day she was pronounced cancer free that *he released her a full year earlier than the standard protocol*. Now THAT is Nahum 1:9! Praise God forevermore.

Vickie now spends much of her time ministering to other women who fight deadly giants. She is a champion. No giant—no champion. No battle—no victory.

I have run all over this globe, preaching, praying, and prophesying. Vickie has stood strong behind me and beside me. No matter how many miles or continents between us, I can feel her strength. I respect and admire all preachers' wives who stand so strong and pay such a dear price to preach the gospel of the Lord Jesus Christ.

Whenever I felt discouraged or overwhelmed with daily duties and challenges, Vickie was always there to encourage me and tell me I could do it and that God would show me the way. What a strength she has been to me.

I have been married to this woman for 47 years. She is my finest disciple. She has no vices and no sin. She has no fake in her at all. What you see in the public is what you get in private. She hates no one. She will go the extra mile or ten to help someone in need. She will tell you the truth in love. She will pray for you. She will cut no corners with you. She will not condemn you, but there is no way she will condone any misbehavior or sin in your life.

Vickie has earned the right to be a spiritual mother to many and has a multitude of daughters in the faith. Her daily devotional has brought insight and strength to many. Her speaking ministry in churches and conferences has straightened out many crooked paths and brought some very biblical insight. Her practical approach to life has stabilized not only our family but many others.

One of Vickie's attributes I admire is her no-nonsense view on life and ministry. She is blunt but not crude. She is straight as an arrow. She always wants to fix broken things, even if you don't welcome her to do so. She is a relentless bloodhound if God puts her on your path.

I have watched God answer Vickie as she prayed over our kids and grandkids. Many things have turned in the right direction because she cried out to God and spoke the Word over our family. God answers her prayers.

Vickie shows no fear. She is just not afraid of you or what you think about her. She is not afraid to travel, even on her own. She has no fear about traveling into foreign lands. She shows no fear of the future.

Vickie is not "Superwoman," but she is a super woman. I have seen her cry. I have seen her when her feelings were hurt and how she got a grip more quickly than most. I have seen her when she is angry. I have seen her when I have made her angry ☺. I have seen her fighting sickness. I have seen her weak and falling in my arms for strength, and I have seen her strong and bold as a lion. I personally wish every woman on the planet could meet her.

She is a well-balanced mixture of a real, down-to-earth woman and spiritual fighter for the family. You don't ever have to locate where she is coming from or what she is trying to tell you. She is very opinionated but will follow my final decision to the tee, even if it's different from hers.

I can remember the two times I was deployed to Vietnam and the look on her face and the embrace she gave me that was to last me almost a year. I watched her as we departed. I wondered each time if I would ever hold her in my arms again. I was hesitant and chose to never ask her what she was thinking. Each time I returned, she was there on the pier, waiting for me. As we came into port, I would be on the flight deck of the aircraft carrier, where I could look over the entire multitude of family members below, waiting for their sailor or Marine to disembark. Out of that multitude I could pick out Vickie every time.

Vickie's children and grandchildren serve the Lord. They are sweet kids. Her husband is known in the city gates. She is an excellent first lady in our ministry. She lives without sin. She pretends to be nothing she's not. She tries to be nobody else. I will spend my life honoring her and holding her yet sharing her with many other people, just as she has done with me. If you ever meet my Vickie, you will never regret it. She is a breath of fresh air and a life changer, and I wish every man's daughter could turn out to be just like her.

11

ME? PREACH?
ARE YOU CRAZY?

It's amazing what one will do when they don't know the Scriptures and they don't understand the kingdom of God or the King of this Kingdom.

I remember the day the Lord told me I was going to preach for Him. "What?" I said. "Me? Preach? Are You crazy?" It's amazing how I could go to Vietnam and face the enemy and the hardships for 21 months without much fear, but when I thought about preaching, I freaked out.

It wasn't like I hadn't spoken in front of people before. I had just spent almost two years as a Marine instructor. I didn't know anything about demons at the time, but I learned later that this was a satanic technique to stop me from obeying God. It brought back a terrible fear from my childhood. I actually remember the day I was supposed to give a book report in high school. It was my turn to stand before the class and read my report. The teacher called my name. I rose and began the walk to the podium. The exit door was to the right of that podium. As I approached the podium, fear gripped me, and I went right out that door and went home!

When the Lord said I would preach for Him, I ran. I never meant to run away from God and my Christianity. I was just running from the thoughts and the fear of becoming a minister. Father always knows best, but when you're a baby Christian, you haven't learned that yet. I sure hadn't.

I was still in the Marines and actually had done very well for myself and intended to make it a career. The day the Lord spoke this to me will live in me forever. He said: "Resign as a U.S. Marine noncommissioned officer, and I will make you a general in My army."

I couldn't see it. I couldn't come to grips with it. I was so overwhelmed, I ran. That's how smart I was in those days. I ran from California to Michigan. I resigned the Marine Corps and was honorably discharged. I found myself in my hometown. Nothing seemed to be right. Nothing fit. I was so miserable. I promised myself that if I ever made it home from the war, I would take a year off and hunt and fish and do nothing but what I wanted to, and that is exactly what I did. But it just wasn't what the Lord wanted for me.

Over a period of nights I had these really strong dreams of what would happen to me if I kept saying no to God. I would wake up in a sweat, yelling out things. In each of these dreams I saw my life under severe attack, my family being disassembled, and my life being slowly destroyed. In dream after dream, night after night, I would be warned by God what would happen if I got out of His will. He showed me how satan would steal my life from me and how I would self-destruct. Not only did this help change the course of Mark Barclay's life, but I have used this many times since to help warn people who get out of the will of God.

In the midst of saying no to God daily, one day I found myself sitting in a lake in Northern Michigan, where I had fallen through the ice. I am a master swimmer and amphibious Marine, but this day was much different. The water wasn't even over my head. If I had been standing it would have only been about knee high. But when I fell through, I slipped, and I was sitting in that freezing water, and the cold got to me quickly. It was a freezing-cold, sub-zero day. The ice started freezing around me. I could feel the onset of frostbite on my exposed skin. The wind chill was horrendous. Being raised in the cold country and knowing the dangers of sub-zero elements, I knew I was in trouble. I was sitting in the water of death. It was only about up to my waist, and normally I would have been able to jump to my feet and find my way to shore before hypothermia could set in, but in this case I couldn't move. My mind raced. I couldn't feel my legs. I felt lethargy set in. I knew I was in deep trouble.

As I struggled to move, I yelled for my friends, but they had driven away to another spot and couldn't even hear me. I was alone. I could feel my heart beating. I kept thinking to myself that I could simply get out of this. I had fallen in northern frozen lakes and rivers before, but this time I couldn't move.

Then God spoke clearly to me: "If you won't preach for Me and obey Me all the days of your life, you will die here today." The power of our flesh and that old stubborn nature are so strong. Even in this condition and not able to move, I still fought to free myself and deny the call. I sat there a moment or two in silence and fear. The Lord spoke again: "So what is it… live, or die? Preach for Me, or die here?"

I suddenly gave up. I gave in. I surrendered to God. "Lord," I said, "If You get me out of this and save my life, I will speak for You all the days of my life." I felt great heat rush through my legs. I could finally move them, and I crawled to the shore and sat shivering and crying out to God, "I will obey You. I will go where You want me to go, and I will speak for You."

As I write this book, forty-some years later, I look back and see that I not only kept my word with the Lord, but He has surely kept His word with me. My life has been spared every step of the way. My family has been spared every step of the way. My ministry has gone global, and most of my preaching friends and colleagues call me "the general." Thank God I was broken before the Lord and obeyed Him.

I have journeyed around the world, preaching the uncompromised Word of God. I have been in the world's great rivers; on mountaintops; and in the jungles, deserts, and cities. I have preached among the tribes and people of every continent. I have established and built churches, Bible schools, missions, and printing centers. I have walked among the largest multitudes to share the gospel of Christ. I have laid hands on so many people for healing and blessing that only Heaven can know the number. I have been blessed to witness Jesus performing many miracles and casting out many demons. It has been a powerful experience to lead many people to Christ and see multitudes filled with the Holy Spirit by the laying on of my hands. Who would have thought that a troubled young man from a small village in Michigan would write so many books and so many magazines that have helped so many people?

Supernatural Ministries Training Institute was God's plan all along. I had no idea I would ever write three years' worth of Bible-college-level curriculum. I would have never guessed nor dreamed I would establish a video school that would reshape the local church and train so many believers in so many countries.

John Osteen once told me that God had used me to bring honor back to the office of the pastor. Only God could have taken a young Marine like me and made me a general in His army. The Lord has sent hundreds of pastors and ministers from all over the world who now call me their pastor, apostle, bishop, mentor, spiritual father, and general.

Thank God, on that day in that lake in the 1970s, I said yes to God and no to Mark.

12

THE VALLEY OF THE SHADOW OF DEATH

I am no stranger to the valley of the shadow of death. I have walked through it many times. I first ran into the "demons of the valley" as a child when the spirit of death got on my dad. I watched him slowly die.

I remember the day of my father's funeral, looking down into the casket and feeling so angry and so betrayed. No, I wasn't mad at my dad. I was just mad.

Demons began to talk to me that day. They drove me. I could feel their evil presence. I couldn't label their influence, and I didn't know what to do with it, being the sinner I was then.

There are certain demons that are at the death site. In fact, Jesus said that death would be the last enemy to die. I can now recognize these evil spirits because I have met them but also because I have the gift of the Spirit called the discerning of spirits (1 Cor. 12:7-12).

I'm not just talking about grief. I'm not just talking about loss. I am referring to the invisible enemy soldiers that fly in and out of the valley of the shadow of death. They see you there, and they want to administer their deadly poison into your soul. If they can get a hook in you, they can drag you anywhere they want, like the ring in the nose of a bull.

VIETNAM—THE VALLEY OF THE SHADOW OF DEATH

I found myself meeting these demons again in the valley of the shadow of death in Vietnam. I fought them for 21 months. Death was everywhere, and we were encircled by it. It overshadowed all of us. I'm not just talking about those who died but the overshadowing spirit of death that brought an invisible gray cloud over all of us. This is exactly what so many veterans deal with as they return home. Many of these demons follow them to harass them the rest of their life.

VICKIE LIVED, AND SO DID JOSH

I found myself in the valley of the shadow of death once again when my wife became pregnant with our son Josh. After having our daughter Dawn, we were told by the doctor to never become pregnant again because of physical issues with Vickie's body. We were told to have no more children, so we didn't plan or purpose to do so. When the doctor said Vickie was pregnant, we had to fight off the fear that came on both of us because of the warnings we had from the medical people.

It was the Lord who planned for us to give birth to another child. I believe this with all my heart. God visited me before Vickie was pregnant with Josh and told me I was going to have a son and to name him Joshua and that he would preach at a young age and help me all the days of my life. I remember telling the Lord that He was talking to the wrong person—that if that's what He wanted, He had better talk to Vickie personally!

When the doctor confirmed the pregnancy, he painted a bleak picture. He turned to me and said, "You're either going to lose your wife or the child." Here came that shadow of death again. It hovered over us.

I know the medical professionals were just doing their job. I'm sure they were a little put out with us because they recommended a full hysterectomy for Vickie, and we refused that surgery. I respected them for their work, but I had a word from Heaven, and that surgery would have negated the promise.

Just before Josh was born, the doctor came out of the delivery room and told me I had to choose between my wife and my baby. We didn't know yet if it was a boy or a girl; things were done differently in those days compared to today. I felt life wanting to drain out of me. That cloud of fear and depression started to sit upon me. That scary, contemptuous gloom was seeping into my soul. Once again I found myself in the valley of the shadow of death. I remember that day clearly, though it seems like a lifetime ago.

As that doctor stood there in front of me, waiting for my answer, his words ran through my soul: "So what is it, son—your wife or your child?" I could feel the special faith rise in me as God's Word overpowered his. God said with a bold, strong voice, "I told you that you *and Vickie* would have a son and you were to name him Joshua, and he would preach at a young age and help you all the days of your life. I did NOT tell you that you only would have a son."

I reached for the doctor and grabbed him and said, "You go back in there, doctor, and you will bring out my son *and* save my wife. Do you understand? God said so."

The next few minutes seemed like days. You see, Vickie's family and mine believed I was a fanatic. Most of them did not believe I heard from God about having a son. So there I stood among them, and all they heard was what the doctor reported.

When that doctor walked out of the surgery room, he was holding my son high to be seen by all. "It's a boy," he said. I wanted to shout, PRAISE GOD! I wanted to turn to the family and shout, I told you so! But first I needed to know about Vickie. I stared into the doctor's eyes with a deep, penetrating, soul-searching combat eye of the tiger, and I could see no fear. He smiled and nodded his head and confirmed that she was okay. *Then* I shouted!

MOM LIVED AND DID NOT DIE

I had an encounter with the spirit of death again when my mom was rushed to ER with heart issues. They said she had a leak, but her age and her health would create quite a risk. I could tell they were thinking of sending her home to eventually die. There isn't room here to tell that whole story, but a great heart surgical team put in "aftermarket" parts (as we hot-rodders would call it), and we took the matter to the altars of God. We anointed Mom with oil and got her baptized in the Holy Ghost. She lived to be 90 years old and still did her own shopping and cooking and had no real health issues. She went to Heaven in total peace and with no struggle. So once again I was in the valley of the shadow of death but delivered by the Lord Jesus Christ.

"YOU WILL NEVER WALK AGAIN"

I was attending Bible college in Los Angeles. My pastor invited us to dinner at his home. We were sitting at the dinner table, and the devil spoke to me and said, "I will stop you now from preaching this gospel." Immediately I was struck in my lower back and fell to the ground. The pain was so severe I could hardly stand it. I couldn't move my legs. I lay on the floor, and once again that weird cloud overshadowed me. The devil said, "You will never walk again—you're finished." Here I was again in the valley of the shadow of death.

The following day my pastor took me to the doctor and then a chiropractor. The x-ray showed that my spine had curved. I heard the words come out of the doctor's mouth, "Were you born this way?" I told him that I had never had any back problems. He began to tell me that he hadn't seen such severe back damage as this in quite a while and wasn't sure he could help me at all. He tried.

I lay at home in bed. I couldn't move without horrible pain. I kept hearing the voice inside of me that I would never walk again. Then I would hear this squeaky, frail voice tell me that by His stripes I am healed. This went on for three days and three nights.

In the middle of the third night something really unusual happened. Something was going on inside of me. This loud voice kept screaming in my head that I would never walk again, that Vickie would not stay with me, and that my life was over. Then this squeaky voice once again would say that by His stripes I am healed. This verse began to repeat over and over again in my head. "So mightily grew the word and prevailed" (Acts 19:20). The war was on!

Back and forth, over and over again, I could hear these two voices within me—a loud voice saying, "You'll never walk again," and that squeaky voice saying, "By His stripes you are healed."

Then something began to happen. That loud, bold voice shouting my defeat with the overshadowing spirit of the shadow of death began to soften. At the same time, that squeaky voice saying I was healed by the stripes of Jesus became bolder. Pretty soon they were of equal volume and equal intensity.

Then suddenly I heard the Word of God shout through my entire soul. With great authority and boldness, the voice of God said, "BY MY STRIPES YOU ARE HEALED!" Then a very, very low-volume, squeaky voice said, "You will never walk again." Immediately my legs were pulled out of that bed as if someone grabbed my ankles and spun me. I jumped to my feet. I stood straight. My back was totally healed. Every symptom was gone. God had given me a miracle, and I've never had a symptom since.

CANCER KILLED—VICKIE LIVES

In Chapter 10, I wrote about the day that my wife Vickie was diagnosed with killer cancer. Wow, talk about walking through the valley of the shadow of death! What a day that was. We are not fakes, and we are not flakes. Ministers feel things, just like you do. We hurt, just like you do. We have to fight off fear and anxiety, just like you do.

I have never been so angry. I wanted to fight and hurt something or somebody. I just couldn't see why such a beautiful person as Vickie would have such an enemy in her body. Once we fought off the fear of this cancer, we formulated our plan of attack. In just over a month Vickie was diagnosed cancer free (1 Cor. 15:57). So once again we walked through this valley, with death overshadowing us, yet it lifted as victory came through Christ.

If you want more of this powerful testimony, get Vickie's daily devotional, *One Day—One Thought—One Year,* or you can get the audio version and hear her tell her story. It is powerful and has helped many people believe that Jesus still heals today.

CANCER KILLED—TRISH LIVES

My daughter-in-law Trish was diagnosed with cancer. We were shocked. This is a girl who watches what she eats, has no vices, no smoking or alcohol use in her past or anything that your mind would associate with such a disease. That terrible dark cloud overshadowed our family once again. Though no one really wanted to say it, we felt the spirit of death trying to bring dismay.

We did what we know to do. We are very grateful that we were taught the uncompromised Word of God and the word of faith. It would again prove to be absolutely true. Today, Trish stands totally free from cancer, and no longer does that shadow of death hover over her or her family. It was another manifestation of the miracle healing power of the Great Master, Jesus Christ, whom we serve.

DROWNED—DIED—RAISED TO LIFE
A DARK DAY IN THE VALLEY OF THE SHADOW OF DEATH

On June 28, 2014, my granddaughter, Jadyn, drowned in the pool. She was underwater for about two minutes, with no breathing for over five.

Jadyn, ten years old at the time, was swimming in the pool, when suddenly she was sucked to the side of the pool—her hair caught in the intake valve. Her little friend Kayla yelled out for help. James, her daddy, was in the pool swimming, when he looked over to see his lifeless baby stuck, not moving, underwater! He got to her and pulled her, literally ripping her hair from the valve, and threw her to the cement pool deck. He began to yell, "Call 911!" and he and a dear friend, Tyler, started working on Jadyn's blue body, all the while yelling, "In the name of Jesus, I command life into this body—no weapon formed against me will prosper." No response, no pulse. This child was not breathing, and her body displayed the other nasty signs of death, according to the ICU professionals.

Her momma, Dawn, stood nearby, battling inside herself and yelling inside, "My child WILL live and NOT die!"

Vickie and I were in a neighboring town at the time, at least 25 minutes from her—and arrived in 12—as we shouted all the way, "Tither's rights, tither's rights, we have tither's rights!" We kept saying, "Not today, devil. We are tithers, and today the God of the tithe will rebuke you, death."

Suddenly life came into Jadyn's body. It was an amazing feeling and sight to see! She began to cough and throw up blood. The EMTs had arrived and began to stabilize her to transport her.

As Dawn slipped into the front seat of the ambulance—blocking out the chatter among the EMTs about Jadyn's stats and her oxygen being dangerously low, breathing for her, and pressing her chest—the driver turned to Dawn and said, "I'll be honest; things aren't looking good." Dawn felt this unusual anger and authority rise up on the inside of her,

"Devil, you DON'T own her, she is NOT yours, she will NOT lose this battle. She's been bought and paid for by the blood of her Jesus, my Jesus, the Creator of life!" And then she said to the EMT, "My God will supply all she needs."

Jadyn came out of the ambulance laughing, and the EMTs were laughing. One said, "She is a very sweet, brave girl. She is a miracle!" Grandpa laid hands on her, and we claimed full victory. No side effects at all. None! Jadyn told us the last thing she remembers before blacking out is asking Jesus to not let her die. After that, the Lord showed her a vision of herself, all grown up.

As she left the hospital, she said, "Mommy, I want out of here. I have to go to church and thank Jesus for listening to me!" She went to church and worshipped at the altar, just four hours after being released. I told the church family that instead of a funeral, we were rejoicing with the Almighty God of the tithe, and also thanked every children's church worker for planting the Word of God in the heart of my children and grandchildren.

Jadyn has no side effects to this day. NONE! She loves swimming and lives in the water at the lake and in the very pool where she drowned. A medical expert who deals with drowning victims told us that we have an extreme miracle—that she lived, and equally miraculous that there are no mental or physical issues. Tithe! Claim tither's rights! Teach your babies to call on the name of Jesus!

Jesus still heals today. If you are facing any physical issues or you have been diagnosed with a deadly disease, I call you healed, in Jesus' name. I pray for you and over you that His healing power manifests in your body and that strength returns to you. May you rise up again and be able to serve your God and take care of your family and live a long, productive life. I curse this disease, in Jesus' name, and I agree with you according to the Holy Scriptures and the work of Calvary that it will go and never return again. I speak peace to your body and to your heart and mind. May you live and not die. May you live long and have a wholesome life.

Meditate in the red letters (the healing verses and words of Jesus), and allow them to bring you hope and strength.

13

MARINE INSTRUCTOR, GOD'S INSTRUCTOR

As a young, barely-19-year-old man I joined the United States Marines. Vickie and I had just been married a few months. The Vietnam War was still in full swing, and I knew I was going to go and fight.

I was a very troubled young man and had not at all recovered from my ugly childhood or my dad's death. I was full of hatred. I wanted to hurt people, and I knew I could do that in the Marines and in the war.

I loved Vickie with all my heart, so much that I couldn't believe I would enlist. I hurt inside with just the very thought of not being with her. She was the one and only person on the planet who brought me peace and made my life worth living.

I was mean and tough and used to fighting. That aggression made me excel in boot camp, and I was a perfect fit in infantry school. I loved the Marine Corps, and I was planning to make it my career. I volunteered for every dangerous job I could find. I wanted to fight, and I wanted to excel at it.

I spent 10 months in Vietnam and came home for about 30 days. Then I volunteered once again, and back we went. In this second tour my life changed forever. I met Jesus Christ after just a few weeks, and I have never turned back.

I not only survived the war zone; I came home a victor, with all my faculties and all my body parts. Okay, we all left something behind. We all came home different. But with Christ I suffered little, and healing came quickly.

I found myself assigned to the Recruit Training Battalion in San Diego as a leader and teacher on the same base where I was trained as a recruit. I would spend the rest of my time in the Corps as an instructor and marksmanship instructor.

I was doing this for a living when God called me into the ministry. As I have testified and explained in an earlier chapter, God told me to resign as a noncommissioned officer in the Corps, and He would make me a general in His army. All I heard in those days was, "Get out of the Marines. Do not reenlist." I knew deep in my heart that my career choice was over. I had no idea what it meant to become a preacher, and I knew even less what it meant to be a general in His army.

I have kept my word with God. He has kept His word with me. For almost five decades I have submitted myself to His will for my life. I left the Marines and have never sought my own will since. Never!

It was God's will for me to be a strong leader in His body. It was His plan for Mark Barclay all along. He knew that. I didn't. I regret nothing. I am ashamed of nothing that God has ever done for me nor the man of God He has built me into today. Nothing!

All I know is that I am not my own and that I have been purchased with a price—a dear price—with the precious blood of the Lamb. I am not my own lord, and I do not call my own shots any longer. I live to do His bidding and carry out His ministry in the earth. Anywhere He has sent me, I have gone. Whatever He has assigned for me to teach and preach, I have done so with full confidence, regardless of its popularity among men.

With all my heart I have endeavored to obey His commands and follow His directions. I will be a preacher and a Christian leader until I take my last breath. Many years ago Vickie and I gave up all our own aspirations and dreams and submitted to His. There is absolutely nothing on our list for the future but to obey Him. If you are not this committed to Christ, I pray you will finally sell out to Him and give Him all. This is His desire for all Christians everywhere, not just a few fivefold ministers.

I went to Bible college and theology school and submitted my life to the elders there to mentor and develop me. I learned early that Christianity is all about developing yourself in the Word and Spirit so you can spend your life developing others. I was set free from bondage and sinful ways so I could help set others free (Matt. 10:8). I was made prosperous so I could teach others how to beat poverty, debt, and lack. I was set free from rage and anger so I could lead others to the foot of the cross so they too can be delivered from such torment. I was taught the Word of God from cover to cover so I could teach others the Word of God from cover to cover (2 Tim. 2:2). I was disciplined and learned the rules and ways of Christ's lifestyle and His kingdom so I could spend my life disciplining others for Christ so they could "follow me as I follow Christ" (1 Cor. 11:1).

I am now known as the "preacher of righteousness." No, I don't see myself as the only one, by any means. Many fivefold ministers call me either the preacher of righteousness or the general. Most of my sons and daughters in the faith refer to me as the general. I never trained them or taught them to do that. It does little or nothing to me or for me. However, when it comes out of their mouth, I am reminded of that day many years ago when I removed my Marine Corps stripes and became a private in this army. I am reminded of the word God gave me to leave and cleave. "Resign from the Corps, and I will make you a general in My army," God said.

In the beginning of our ministry we thought no one would ever invite us to speak. Now we can't fulfill all the global requests. In the beginning we knew nothing about ministry. Now we are called upon by thousands of ministers for help, to bring wisdom, and to advise. In the beginning we were fairly stationary and hardly had anywhere to go. Now we are on every inhabited continent in the world. In the beginning we devoured books and spent sleepless nights studying and researching. Now we write books, curricula, and magazines. In the beginning we decided that we would obey God all the days of our lives, and we are still on that course.

I will share with you here the "stays" that Vickie and I have learned and live by:

1. Stay submitted to a leader whom you will obey.

2. Stay out of sin—ALL sin, all the time.

3. Stay in the Word all the days of your life.

4. Stay in church, no matter what.

5. Stay coming to the altar of God and falling at the feet of Calvary.

6. Stay humble and teachable.

7. Stay a tither and giver—no matter what the devil says, no matter what people say, and no matter what your circumstances say.

8. Stay the course.

I am now a leader among men. Many who serve in governments around the world call upon me. Many who are in judicial positions and law enforcement call upon me. Many ministers of the gospel call upon me. I have a national telecast, and I have an international video Bible school. I have my own publishing company. I have missionaries all over the globe. I have many pastors and churches submitted to me and Mark Barclay Ministries. I have a multitude who now look to me and call me their father in the faith, dad, pastor, apostle, bishop, and yes, *general*.

It's all God, it is totally by God, and it is to the glory of God. Just think about it… God takes a very poor, very hurt and angry young man and saves him, delivers him, and disciplines him… and here we are. I cannot even begin to tell you how much God and His generals invested in me as I grew and followed His destiny for my life.

Today I write this book (one of many) as an Ephesians 4:11 fivefold ministry gift. I still love the Marine Corps, and I go to as many bases and minister to as many Marines as I can. But I am of a much higher rank now and in a much larger army, God's army—a general in God's army, just like He said.

14

GIANTS IN THE LAND

Some of the greatest stories in the Bible are the ones where the men of God take on the enemy giants and defeat them. After all these years of reading and studying the Bible, I still get pumped when I read them and preach from those passages.

I never saw preachers as anything but cookie-nibbling, tea-sipping sissies. I have no idea why, because I didn't really know any and wasn't raised in church. I had no idea how tough most of them are or how many mighty feats they conquer and win.

As a former Marine warrior, I have great respect for the man who, without modern weapons, picked up the jawbone of a donkey and took on enemy soldiers (Judges 15:15-16). How about Paul and Silas, who were beaten by the government police and thrown into a dark, damp, bacteria-infested dungeon inhabited by rats and bugs? Or what about this disciple of Christ and preacher, Peter? He lay shackled between two government guards who were to take him to receive the death penalty the very next day. Nerves of steel? Sure. Why? Because he wasn't old yet, and he remembered the words Jesus spoke over him that "when he was old" young men would lead him by the hand. That hadn't occurred yet, so he sleeps and has rest in his soul that no matter what the circumstances dictated, he was going to be freed and go on with his ministry because Jesus said so (John 21:18).

As I grew in Bible knowledge, I began to realize that not all giants in the land were huge in size or wicked inside. These men were giants, and there are many more. God's enemies learned that His men and women would not bow, whether it was the three Hebrew children in the furnace, or the Book of Acts believers, refusing to be quiet or stop spreading the gospel.

I don't know if you have ever really studied much about martyrs or how the early apostles died, refusing to compromise their belief in Christ. I will share my findings with you. This list proved to me that these preachers and disciples were tough—very tough!

- Matthew was slain with a sword at Ethiopia.

- Mark was cruelly dragged through the streets in Alexandria.

- Luke was hanged upon an olive tree in Greece.

- John was put in a caldron of boiling oil but miraculously escaped death and was banished to Patmos.

- James the Greater was beheaded at Jerusalem.

- James the Less was thrown from a lofty pinnacle of the temple and then beaten to death with a fuller's club.

- Peter was crucified upside down at Rome.

- Bartholomew was flayed alive.

- Andrew was bound to a cross, whence he preached to his persecutors until he died.

- Thomas was run through the body with a lance at Coromandel in the East Indies.

- Paul, after various tortures and persecutions, was at length beheaded at Rome by the emperor Nero.

- Barnabas of the gentiles was stoned to death at Salonica.

- Jude was shot to death with arrows.

- Matthias was first stoned and then beheaded.

…and the list of these great, courageous soldiers of the cross goes on and on and on!

I was blessed to have Kingdom generals and fathers in my life. Up until recently, when my one remaining father in the faith went home to Heaven, I had never been without a key leader in my life. Let me give you a short version of each of these great men who used the anointing on their life and the Word of God to form and shape Mark Barclay to be what he is today.

The first is my first pastor, Bill Falling. He told me he was an expert disciple maker, and if I would be worth investing in, he would make me a disciple of Jesus Christ. He did, and I am. I received every discipline, correction, rebuke, and teaching he gave me, and I took it to heart. He and that first church helped me receive my deliverance from many things. It was called Faith Center but actually, to me, it was "Freedom" Center. He was a good pastor, and he helped me very much. I will be forever grateful.

Pastor John Osteen (a Spirit-filled, tongue-talking, demon-casting-out man of God; a miracle healer in Christ; and a global missionary) built a church of about 20,000 members without cheating at all or using any marketing schemes. He was a holy man and in love with Jesus Christ. He could say more in 30 minutes from the pulpit than most do in 90. He changed the world, and he changed me. In my final meeting with him he asked me what I wanted from him and why I chased him for almost 30 years. I answered, "Pastor, I don't want anything *from* you, I want to be *like* you" (Heb. 6:12).

Dr. Kenneth E. Hagin was a true prophet of God and one of the best Bible teachers I have ever met. He literally changed the world with his teaching on faith. He helped develop the future through his prophetic gift and flowing in the gifts of the Spirit. He sure changed me. Many,

many ministers of the gospel and believers are obeying God today because of his obedience to our Lord and Savior. My life was marked forever by sitting in his meetings, where Jesus would show up.

I'm not sure I ever met a man more in love with truth and God's Word than Dr. Roy Hicks. I knew him from the '70s until he got promoted to Heaven in 2008. His tenacity to study and interrogate the Holy Scriptures has stuck with me to this day. I am a great student of the Bible because of him. He creased the life of so many young ministers and for decades kept most of the Church out of heresy and false doctrines. He sure changed my life.

Dr. George Evans was a supernatural prophet of God. He was given one of the most accurate prophetic gifts I have ever witnessed. He was in love with Jesus Christ and the ministry of Jesus Christ. I had the privilege of following his lead for four decades of my life. He read the Bible through more times than anyone I know. He built a great missionary Bible school and sent out many students, including me. He has disciples all over the world. He taught me how to pray and to always give an altar call. "Word, worship, workshop," he would say.

Dr. Lester Sumrall was a man of no comparison. He was a guru when it came to the supernatural realm, angels, and demons. He was afraid of no one. He spoke the truth in a way that no one could misunderstand him. He was absolutely a general in God's army. I learned so much from him, especially in our private times—so much so, that many say I sound like him and stand like him. God used him to keep the body of Christ stable for many years. He literally changed the world with his Feed the Hungry program and the many books he wrote. I still read them to this day. He was a man who walked with God.

Healing evangelist Tommy Lee Osborn was truly a nation changer, from his simplified teaching and call to salvation to the gift of miracles God imparted to him. His books and preaching won many to Christ and realigned many Christians and drew them back to Calvary. The day I met him was a day I will remember all my life. I was privileged to follow him and his ministry. My pastor, John Osteen, said he was the finest and most potent missionary he had ever met. I concur.

Dr. Oral Roberts changed the entire world with his teachings and sayings. His miracle healing ministry alone saved multitudes of people from dying of diseases and living in pain. I will never forget this saying: "Something good is about to happen to you today." Or how about this one: "Expect a miracle." I have literally lived my life after his teachings on seedtime and harvest. When he told me to read Matthew, Mark, Luke, and John four times through on my knees, it sowed the truths of Christ and the ministry of Jesus deep into my heart forever. His very stature and commitment to Christ changed my life, and I will never turn back.

Dr. Hilton Sutton was a very kind man yet very strong in dealing with people. He saw no reason to compromise, and he taught the Bible with authority. He became known as one of the greatest Bible prophecy teachers ever. I will always cherish the times we had together. He helped me understand the end times and what to look for next. One of his most famous quotes was: "These modern preachers have lost track of God in His own house and do not know how to get Him back, so they have opted for other things to attract people."

I am so very blessed to have known each of these men of God. I am what I am because of the influence and impartation they made in my life.

I was introduced by the host of a very large conference, who said: "You are about to hear from Osteen, Sumrall, Hicks, Evans, Sutton, Roberts, Hagin, and others who imparted so much into Brother Barclay!"

MY SENIOR PICTURE   VICKIE'S SENIOR PICTURE

OUR FIRST HOUSE—JUST MARRIED

MY FIRST JOB—SELLING POPCORN AT BUDD THEATER

MY GRANDPA'S FARM
WHERE I MILKED COWS BY HAND
AND LEARNED TO HUNT AND TRAP

TREES I TRIMMED
WHEN I WAS A CHILD...
NOW THEY'RE GROWN

OUR WEDDING IN 1970

OUR 25TH WEDDING CEREMONY

ALIVE AND WELL IN 2016

FORTY-SEVEN YEARS TOGETHER

MY VICKIE
HEALED OF CANCER
IN 32 DAYS

PRAYING AT THE VIETNAM WALL, WASHINGTON, DC,
GRATEFUL MY NAME IS NOT ON IT!

I WAS A SERIOUS MARINE
TO RECKON WITH

I WAS A MARINE INSTRUCTOR,
RECRUIT BATTALION, SAN DIEGO

I WORKED AT EDSON RANGE
AS A MARINE INSTRUCTOR

MY DRESS BLUES

EISENHOWER COMMISSION

I SPENT 21 MONTHS IN VIETNAM

OUR FAMILY

AT OUR U.S. CAPITOL
IN 2014

PREACHING TOGETHER WITH MY VICKIE

PREACHING TOGETHER
WITH MY SON-IN-LAW JAMES

PREACHING TOGETHER
WITH MY DAUGHTER DAWN

PREACHING TOGETHER WITH MY SON JOSH

REACHING MILLIONS
THROUGH TV

WORLDWIDE WEBINAR AND COMMUNION SERVICE

THE MBM TELECAST HAS AIRED FOR DECADES

HAVING FUN PREACHING

**SHOOTING OUR VIDEO
BIBLE COLLEGE, SMTI**

ANGEL 1 DELIVERING THE PROPHET TO THE NATIONS

I'VE BEEN AROUND THE WORLD MANY TIMES

MY FRIEND,
SENATOR RICK SANTORUM

PRAYER FOR SENATOR TED CRUZ

DR. LESTER SUMRALL, MY SON JOSH, AND ME

MINISTERING TO MINISTERS

I WAS CHOSEN BY PAT SUMMERALL
AS AN AMERICAN SUCCESS STORY

MY PASTOR OF 27 YEARS,
DR. JOHN OSTEEN

MY FRIEND, KENNETH COPELAND

ONE OF MY FATHERS IN THE
FAITH, DR. LESTER SUMRALL

ONE OF MY FATHERS IN THE FAITH, DR. ROY HICKS

MY FIRST PASTOR,
BILLY FALLING

MY FATHER IN THE FAITH,
DR. GEORGE EVANS

MY FATHER IN THE FAITH,
DR. HILTON SUTTON

15

ME? TV?
ARE YOU KIDDING ME?

THE TOOL MAN

Many of my preaching colleagues and sons and daughters in the faith have called me "the tool man." I learned many years ago from the Marines that there is a tool for every task, and if you have that tool, you work faster and easier and don't botch up everything. If you have to accomplish the task without the right tools, you never do as well, and you're certainly not as efficient. Even the Bible tells us that if the ax-head is dull, it takes more strength or much more effort (Eccles. 10:10).

While we were pioneering, back in the early '80s, there was a time we had very little. Sometimes Vickie and I never even got paid. Our church owned very little (steel folding chairs and a rented room at the Jaycee Hall). But I remember putting a big board up on the wall, and every service we would all point to it and claim that one day we would be able to make copies of cassettes and print books. Man, were we dreaming!

I still remember our first recorder and our first duplicating machine. We were blessed. I boasted of God's goodness to everyone. We were "big time" and not only that, we had raised enough money to buy an overhead projector. In case you weren't a churchgoer in the late '70s and early '80s, we needed projectors to display the song lyrics on the wall (or if you were rich, on an actual screen). We were "wall people" for quite some time.

I also remember our first wireless microphone. I believe it was from Radio Shack. We were giants now! Are you kidding me—no more wires to trip over, and no more stands to carry around? The only problem with it (well, not the only problem) was that it cut out so often it was fairly worthless and very annoying. No offense to the manufacturer, but the technology just wasn't around yet. It also sometimes picked up a truck driver, talking on his radio as he passed by on our freeway ramp, and it would go through our speakers and pretty much cut me out. Usually it was clean language, but sometimes we just stopped and prayed for that driver to get saved. The truth is, we didn't need a microphone at all, let alone a fancy wireless one. I mean, we were about 45 people strong. My Marine Corps instructing voice could easily reach a group that small.

I can still remember our first IBM electric typewriter. (If you're under 40, don't worry about that illustration—it would take too long to explain!) The day I got my first personal computer was so exciting. It was a portable Macintosh SE/30. (Well, it was barely portable.) It was about twice the size of my briefcase, but the screen could be covered by my hand. Nonetheless, it was a new tool, and I was flying high.

**MY FIRST COMPUTER,
THE APPLE MACINTOSH PORTABLE
16 POUNDS, 16 MHz, 1 MG RAM,
9.8-INCH SCREEN**

Speaking of flying high… I was on a commercial flight for an overseas missions trip, and the host paid for me to be seated in first class. You should have seen the others seated around me and heard all the chatter when I broke out that portable computer. No one had seen one before.

Even the pilots took turns coming out of the cockpit to see it. (It was much easier for them to do that in those days!) The man sitting next to me offered to pay me if I would let him play with it for a few minutes. I reluctantly allowed it—not the payment, just to hold it and appreciate it. I didn't charge him. The look in his eyes was payment enough.

OUR FIRST AIRPLANE

In late 1981, I was speaking at Living Word International Outreach Center (our home church in Midland, Michigan) when a man raised his hand from the congregation and wouldn't lower it. He finally said, "Pastor, I have something I must say to this congregation." I answered swiftly, "I'm sorry, but we do not do that here in this church, but you can talk to me after the service." He answered with a "Yes, sir," and I continued to finish my Sunday morning message.

As I was giving my third closing (it seems every good preacher has at least three), he actually stood up in the congregation and said, "Please, Pastor, God sent me here to say something to this congregation, and I think you will want to hear it." I motioned for the ushers to remove him from the service, and I was just speaking my first couple words to more sternly tell him to be seated and be quiet, when the Holy Spirit said, "Let him speak; I sent him here today."

I called him forward and informed him that he had only a couple minutes. He politely thanked me and had such respectfulness about him. He didn't address me so much but turned to the congregation and said, "You will lose this pastor you love dearly. [I almost took the mic from his mouth.] God is going to promote him to an international level and make him a general in His army. He will need to be gone much, and he will see you little. Jesus sent me here to tell you that you need to buy an airplane… not to send him out but so he can get home more often."

An airplane, I thought. Wow, whoever thought of an airplane. I never did. I was still trying to meet the weekly bills and hope there was enough left to pay my salary. At that time I didn't even know I would be traveling much. But within minutes, there was all kinds of money being placed at the altar. I tried to stop it. My "stranger guest" was not receiving an offering, and neither was I. It was spontaneous. It was immediate. One man came up to me and said, "I have some land I'm selling; I will donate all that money to the plane. I don't want to lose you. You are the best pastor I have ever had." Another was selling a building, and on and on it went. In a matter of about 20 minutes that little church of about 75 people (counting everyone, including the church mouse) had given about $165,000! I was speechless. I was also very happy that I knew the voice of God, because the same man I was going to have removed from the sanctuary was the man Jesus sent to buy our first plane.

Somewhere in the midst of this supernatural giving, this visiting stranger left the sanctuary unbeknownst to me. His gift was cash in an unmarked envelope. I have no idea who he was, and I have never seen him since.

I bought that airplane and called Dr. Lester Sumrall (one of my dads) and told him what had happened. He said, "Fly that plane over here, son, and let me see it." We did, and he acted like it was the best plane he had ever seen. It wasn't. In fact, compared to the LeSea jet (his ministry aircraft), it was but a squirt. He came aboard that plane and blessed it. He christened it and told me it would be just the first of many planes that God would give me to preach this gospel and that I was to call each future plane into the ministry of Jesus Christ. I have done that for every plane my ministry has purchased.

I realize that most people have no idea why a preacher needs an airplane. It isn't a luxury item, and it isn't a Hollywood thing. It is, for many of us, a mandatory tool. Many critics to God's Word have no issues with the porn peddler, adulterer, booze peddler, etc., having an airplane. In fact, they think it's awesome and a sign of great success. But they have a tremendous problem if a plane is used to propagate God's Word and reach the unreached and tell the untold.

We have studied many times how our ministry and church could accomplish our mission without the plane. Each and every time we come up with the same conclusion. We cannot! I would have to resign my pastorate, disobey God in my bishopric to many ministers, and discontinue my oversight of these many, many churches. We would have to literally eliminate about 65 percent of all my preaching appointments, let alone all the other ministry-related trips to help rescue churches and pastors.

You see, commercial airlines are overwhelmed and cannot get me to two or three cities a day. That's right, sometimes I speak in three cities or states in one day. Many, many times I have spoken in one state in the morning and a different state in the evening. This is pretty much impossible on commercial airlines (no offense to them).

TV

I never, ever had the thought or the desire to be on TV. I am still not sure it is my strength, but I do it because my God told me to. I have been doing it now for quite a few years, both nationally and locally.

When the Lord Jesus told me to take the message that burns in my heart and distribute it to this generation with every means available to me by God, He had included television, but I had not. When the Lord first told me to do television, I about fell down. I sort of pretended that I didn't hear Him. Of course I knew I had, and He knew I had, and I knew I had been had!

I told my son Josh, who has been my sidekick all of his life, that we were going on TV. He immediately responded with something like, "How can we do that? Who will do that for us? Where will we get the equipment to do this?"

My answer was, "All I know is that God wants us to do it, and we are going to find a way to do it." After a few days of prayer, God said to tell Josh that he was to take on this project and find out what to buy and buy it. He was 15 years old at the time. That's right—15 years old! He investigated everything and brought me the equipment list and the bills. Wow! I almost fell to the ground. "Josh," I said, "Did you pick out all the most expensive items, or what?" He informed me that he hadn't— that he picked out mid-range equipment rather than the very cheapest. I appreciated that, but I had no idea from where such a large amount of money would come.

I do know this: With everything God has ever told me to do, I started with no money at all. This seemed to be no different. It would take an absolute intervention of God. But God and His people showed up again. (That's another story for another day.)

The equipment arrived in big boxes on a big truck, and Josh asked me what to do with it. I remember telling him to stack all the boxes in the corner of the sanctuary, and I would pray about what to do with all of it. When I prayed, the Lord said, "I will anoint Josh to figure it out, put it all together, and make it work. Then I will anoint him to produce the program, edit it, and get it to the stations." I remember saying to the Lord, "What stations? There are no stations. I have never done TV before. Lord, we don't even know how to get on a station."

"I want you to have Josh put all this together and record and practice for one year. After that year I will show him and you what to do." Well, we did, He did, and we are now reaching multitudes by television. We have graduated thousands of students from our video Bible college. We are in our fourth generation of equipment. We now have a state-of-the-art TV suite and first-class equipment. Thank You, Jesus, and thank you, Josh.

When I first told Josh to order that equipment, it was thousands and thousands of dollars. I still remember the day that I told Josh (at 15 years old) that God was going to anoint him to put all that equipment together and make it work. His answer was, "Dad, are you crazy? I don't know how to do all that. Have you forgotten that I'm only a teenager?" I said, "Don't they come with manuals?" (This was before you could go on the Internet and watch a YouTube video or tutorial.) But he took the challenge and opened all those boxes, and with God's anointing, he made it all work. Now he helps many other ministries, consulting with them about their video and audio projects.

As for us, we work hard, night and day, to obey our God and reach the unreached and tell the untold. We will inexhaustibly, and with every means available to us by God, prepare His people for His coming, bring a move of the Holy Spirit to all people of this generation, and provide leadership to leaders and future leaders, both in the local church and in the marketplace, including government, the judicial system, education, business, military, and law enforcement—so help me, God!

16

WORLD MISSIONS

In 1977 I met a man named George Evans. He was the pastor of Bible Missionary Temple in San Diego and founder of Berean Bible College. He was a true prophet of the Lord and sold-out missionary. I had no idea when I met him that he would become one of my closest friends and fathers in the faith. We preached together for over three decades before he went to be with the Lord.

I loved his love for the Word of God, and I personally know no one who has read the Bible through more than he. But it was his commitment to world missions that turned me into a world missionary myself. With his influence in my life I have traveled the world over.

Then I met John Osteen. Pastor Osteen was totally consumed with missions. He was absolutely contagious. It fueled my tank, and I couldn't seem to go often enough. I was driven. I intensified my journeys and found myself constantly thinking about where to go next. I put a globe next to the chair in my den, and I would spend hours praying over it until the Lord spoke to me where to go next and how to do it.

In the 1980s I met another man of God who would change my life forever. Dr. Lester Sumrall was a master missionary and an absolute guru on the supernatural. He was so authoritative. He reminded me of an old general in the Marines. He was so focused and so committed to go where God wanted him to go.

I have never lost this drive for world missions. It rests deep in my heart. To this day I am totally involved in reaching the world. "Reaching the unreached and telling the untold" has become a theme of our life and ministry. I have been on every continent at one time or another. I have been to the mountaintops and in the major cities. I have been up the Amazon and down under to Australia and New Zealand. I have preached in the desert, and I have preached in the jungle. Wherever the Lord has commanded me to go, I have gone. Whether it took a jet, car, snow machine, canoe, or camel, I have never said no to Jesus, and I have never flinched, even if the assignment was going to be tough.

I have slept in the finest hotels and with the bugs and frogs. I have eaten in the world's finest restaurants and also with natives where I would swear things were moving in my bowl. I have been to the highest security compounds and in the most dangerous of all places.

One time I was in Guatemala with a couple helpers. We were staying on a military compound outside of Guatemala City. While there, a communist-backed, military-level force attacked the city and also our barracks. We were under fire for some time. Bullets were rattling through our housing, and explosions were going off all around us. I remember telling the other two men with me to crawl under their bunk and put their mattress on top of them and stay as flat to the floor as they could. I informed them that I was not dying there in Guatemala, and I would actually fight if I had to.

We all began to pray in tongues and speak Psalm 91 protection over our lives and summon the angels. In the middle of the night we heard even louder explosions and more intense gunfire. I knew that meant there was a firefight outside our barracks.

I heard heavy footsteps coming down our hallway. Whoever it was, they headed right for us. As those steps got closer and louder, I knew they were either police boots or military. In this case they were military. We had barricaded the door and were just at the level of anxiety where you could hear your heart beating within you, when a voice yelled "U.S. missionaries… U.S. missionaries… we are here to transport you to the airport and safety." Being military minded, I was suspicious but yelled back, "Who are you, and why should I listen to you?" His reply was loud and strong as he announced his name, rank, and serial number. He said he was Guatemalan army and that time was crucial. I trusted him and the confidence I heard in his voice.

They ran us down a long hallway and out a side door into military vehicles. The small arms fire was still going off, but no bullets were flying around us anymore. As we drove away, I looked back and gave thanks that we were okay and whatever trap satan had set for us, he failed once again. Jesus is Lord, and He was with us, and the angels surrounded us that night. Thanks be unto God!

We made it to the aircraft, and they ushered us right on with no tickets or anything. "Sit here!" they said. First class. Works for me! Just two or three minutes later a U.S. ambassador ran up the stairs and hurried on the plane and sat next to me. The door closed immediately, and the plane started taxiing before the door was even sealed and locked. He introduced himself to me and asked what I was doing in Guatemala. He informed me that things were not all good and that he was grateful we also got out and got on the plane safely for the United States.

I was able to visit with my two friends and ask them if they were okay. They were fine and said they were grateful they were with me and thankful for what they were taught about God's protection. The younger one looked like he may never go on the mission field again. The older, more seasoned gentleman said we'd go back there one day and save a lot of souls. We did go back, more than once through the years. We won a lot of souls, and we helped build and strengthen the churches and missionaries. And yes, the young man also returned with us more than once.

In the 1980s I took a trip to Africa up into the Igbo Tribe region. I did not verify this, but their chief told me they had not seen a white man in decades and that he could not remember in his lifetime having a white preacher come there to tell them about the things of God.

It was very hot there. It had been so dry for so long that when we stepped on the ground to walk, it caused dust clouds around our feet. The dirt was almost a reddish color. When I got home, I could not get the dirt out of my clothing. Every place that I had sweat (which was just about everywhere) was stained. It was so hot I was never able to quench my thirst. I think I perspired from the time I got there until we were a good hour in the air on the way home with the air conditioner blowing on me.

The conditions were miserable, but sometimes that's what it takes to reach remote areas and preach the gospel to the entire planet. Even sleeping was miserable with no air conditioning, no fans inside the windows, and only a piece of canvas for a door. We showered each night by pouring water out of a bucket over each other's heads. Sometimes that water was actually from the river. Yippee.

We were preaching for an evening crusade and doing morning teachings for whoever was there. I was shocked at how many people came from so far away and how many would stand in that massive crowd in that kind of heat so they could hear the Word of God preached and see Jesus perform miracles. We were resting one afternoon in a little tent. As we were praying in the Holy Ghost, the Lord said to go down to the end of a certain dead-end road and find a trail and follow it. When I told my missionary friend what I thought the Lord was telling me to do, he tried to talk me out of it. I don't blame him for that—we were beat. It was hot. We were dirty, we were thirsty, and we still had a day or two to go.

He decided to go with me. I decided I was doing it if it took all day. I was going to obey God, even if I had to go alone. We got an interpreter and a driver and headed in the direction God said. But when we got to the dead-end road, there was no trail. All four of us looked around the vehicle, on the road, and into the side ditches and found nothing.

My friend was looking at me like I was crazy and perhaps had totally missed God. But when I was just about ready to submit to this idea, the interpreter yelled out, "I think I found a trail." There it was, and we started our march through the jungle. I still had no idea where I was going or what I was going to do when I got there.

After we walked a while, I began to hear a noise. I knew it was people. We walked on. It got louder and louder because obviously we were getting closer and closer. As we walked on, I began to recognize it as singing, though I could not understand the language and I did not know the song. As we came upon this place, I could now recognize with my eye and knew deep in my heart why God stirred us to do this.

It was shocking! I had a rush of emotions from anger to sympathy, when I saw a young lady, perhaps in her early twenties, who was literally shackled to a tree. She was bound with something like logging chains and steel shackles, and she was attached to that tree. The tree had been stripped and was basically a pole still rooted in the front yard of this little shack. I could tell she'd been there for a while because the ground was beaten down in a circle like what a dog might do if he was tied to a tree for a long time. She had such a tormented, evil, horrible, and fearful look in her eyes and on her face.

I guess the keeper of the home could hear us talking and came running out of his little shack. He was talking to us through the interpreter. I yelled at him to let this lady go free. He refused. I commanded him once again. He looked very afraid and refused. Finally he identified himself as the person who not only owned the little shack but the pastor of that small gathering of people. That's why they were singing. He explained to me that the girl tied to the tree was his daughter, and if he let her go free, she would run into the fire or into the river and try to kill herself. They had tried many times to allow her to live in the house, but she ran away and would outrun her parents, driven by this demon and by suicide, and they could not catch her.

Immediately the Lord spoke to me and said, "This demon has met Me, and I cast him out; remember, son?"

MATTHEW 17:14-18

And when they were come to the multitude, there came to him a *certain* man, kneeling down to him, and saying, Lord, have mercy on my son: for he is lunatick, and sore vexed: for ofttimes he falleth into the fire, and oft into the water. And I brought him to thy disciples, and they could not cure him. Then Jesus answered and said, O faithless and perverse generation, how long shall I be with you? how long shall I suffer you? bring him hither to me. And Jesus rebuked the devil; and he departed out of him: and the child was cured from that very hour.

As I was listening to the Lord, a holy indignation came up from within me. With a much more authoritative voice, I commanded this man to take the shackles off his daughter. For some reason, this time he did it. The moment those shackles came off, we grabbed that girl and cast that demon out. She shook and squirmed and foamed at the mouth. She fell as though dead. But in a matter of moments, she jumped to her feet and began to shout praises to our Lord Jesus Christ.

We had her bathed and her hair done pretty and bought her clothes. We took her to the crusade meeting, and when she came to the platform, the whole multitude ignited with awe and began to shout praises to God. In the moments that followed, we saw more healing miracles and demonstrations of the Almighty God than I had ever seen before. Everyone in that whole region knew this girl and was familiar with her shackles. God knew this, and He knew to send my partner and me to that tree in the jungle. The deliverance of that girl spread far and wide and is probably still being preached and talked about to this day.

She was free. She stayed free. I heard reports years later that she is not only free but helping others get free from binding and hindering spirits. I will be forever grateful that the Lord used us this way.

I CAST OUT THE DEMONS THAT DROVE HER TO THE FIRE AND TO THE RIVER TO KILL HER

I remember a trip to the mountains near Tacoa in Honduras. Our trip was to be about a week long, and we were going to be in three different cities. When we arrived, we were led to go to the mountains to help a native pastor who was having horrible problems there. The communist aggressors were actually attacking some of the pastors as they were dismissing their church services and would kill them with a machete, right in front of their people. This pastor said he could not get anyone to come to help him. His people were also terrified and wanted to close the church.

When we arrived in the little mountain village, it was just about dark. At about 10 p.m. I stood in the public square and yelled at the devil, "Come after us, you coward. Come out now, and we will cast you out." This went on for quite some time, and no one came. Not a person.

We finally went back to the house where we were staying. When we got there, one of the family members had recently died, and the husband was trying to prepare her body for burial but became deadly sick from Formaldehyde fumes. He was actually unconscious and slowly dying. We went into the room and laid hands on him and commanded him to come alive. He slowly woke up but couldn't really speak. Within an hour he was off that bed, walking out of that room, and speaking clearly. What a great miracle Jesus did for us that night.

Just for the record, the killers never returned to the village or neighboring villages. The believers began to gather again, and the churches not only stayed open but began to grow. Praise God!

The next day as we were settling for the night, just before 10 p.m., the Lord spoke to me to move our team immediately. I had just lain down on the pads on the floor (my bed for the night) with my head on my shepherd's bag (which I was using as my pillow). I was so tired, and I knew my team was as well, but I learned long ago to just obey the Lord and follow His lead.

I gave the command to pack up and get to the bus station. They did it but in a somewhat protesting manner. We all packed quickly and headed for the depot. It was walking distance, and when we got there, only one man was there, and he was about to close the depot.

When we arrived at the bus depot, the man working there informed us in no uncertain terms that there would be no more buses that night. From outside the depot office I watched him converse with my interpreter. My interpreter finally came out and informed me of this. I sent him back in to tell the clerk there was going to be a bus tonight because God told me to go to La Ceiba, and that is where we were going. As you can imagine, the conversation went on for quite a few minutes, with my interpreter going in and coming out of that office with the same report. The clerk kept telling us that the last bus left before dark, and there would not be another one until morning. He was sure of it. They did not travel that route after dark because it was too dangerous of a drive, and there were too many bandits.

It was going on midnight, and the other missionaries with me were beginning to give me that look as if I missed God. I know they were trying hard not to challenge me, but I could tell they wanted to. Even I was beginning to feel weak about the whole thing. I was wrestling inside myself about whether or not I heard from God. I kept reassuring myself that God spoke to me, and I knew His voice that well.

It was just a few minutes after midnight when I saw headlights coming and shining through the tree line. As they got closer, I could tell it was a bus. And yes, believe it or not, it was pulling into the depot and finally stopped right in front of us. It was a newer Mercedes bus, and it was full of people. I grabbed the interpreter and stepped on the bus before the driver could get off. "Where are you headed?" I asked. Sure enough, he was headed for La Ceiba. The man running the depot was now also in the doorway of the bus. He looked pretty confused and a little alarmed. He asked the driver to explain why he was there, and the explanation went like this: "Somewhere, somehow, I made a wrong turn earlier in the evening and couldn't find my way back to the main road until just a little bit ago. I stopped here so you could call down to La Ceiba (this was before cell phones and GPS devices) and let them know we're okay and that we are still coming." There was no lodging there for all those people so, dangerous or not, they had to push on.

I asked the driver if the bus was full or if he could handle three more passengers. I had my money in my hand and was ready to pay him extra, even if we had to stand in the aisle. I knew God sent this bus, and there was no way I wasn't going to be on it. I had no idea what was so urgent and why God wanted us in La Ceiba, but we were bound to be there.

I was looking intently throughout the bus for open seats and also for anyone I could pay to give up their seat. The driver got up out of his seat and walked to the back of the bus. He returned and said, "THERE ARE ONLY THREE SEATS left on the bus." Uncanny? No, supernatural! I paid him some American money, which was more than a month's pay for him. Everyone was happy. My friends were blown away, the depot manager was absolutely speechless, and I was feeling pretty spiritual!

When we arrived in La Ceiba, we scrambled to our rooms and headed for showers and our beds. We were physically beat. It was now about 3 a.m. At around 5 a.m. I was awakened to hard rapping on the door. I got up to see what was the matter. It was a representative from a group of ministers who were meeting at 7 a.m. and wanted me to come to speak to them. "No way," I said. "That is not going to happen. Maybe in the afternoon or evening, but not that early." I explained that we had just settled in. They said, "We know, we already got word from Tacoa of the miracles in the churches, the miracle with the person dying from Formaldehyde poisoning, and the miracle of the bus appearing. We must have you come." I responded again with a firm "no" and returned to my rack.

As I was falling back asleep, I felt the anointing of God come upon me, and He said, "You be there at 7 a.m. I am going to use you to change this country." Dead tired or not, I would be there as the Lord commanded. And I was. As hungry as we were, we opted out of breakfast in trade for another 30 minutes of sleep. As I arrived in the meeting, they immediately introduced me as the man with the miracles from the mountains of Tacoa.

As I began to speak, there was a commotion among the fifty or so people in room. It got so loud that I asked the interpreter what was happening. After he conversed with the ministers, he reported to me that they wanted me to teach on the baptism in the Holy Spirit and speaking in tongues (one of my favorite topics). I was excited and intrigued all at the same time. "Who are these people?" I asked. They were bishops, superintendents, and overseers of different non-Spirit-filled churches, including the Mennonites and other denominations. They were here for a summit meeting and heard of the happenings in the mountains. They wanted me to help them to be filled with this level of the power of God so they too could operate at that level in the supernatural.

As I stood there, it became very clear why God wanted me to get out of Tacoa and get to La Ceiba. This was it. By high noon every one of those bishops, apostles, supervisors, and overseers was filled with the Holy Spirit and spoke with other tongues. What a miracle meeting. Well, the rest of the story goes on and on as these leaders went home and taught on the baptism and led most of their congregational members in this same infilling of the Holy Spirit. In fact, on the next trip there, I spoke at a large Mennonite church, and they were all speaking in tongues.

God is so good. I was preaching in Olavarría, Argentina, south of Buenos Aires, with my dear friend, Jorge Bardey, when the Lord pointed out a man to me I had never met. I called him out from that large crowd of people and began to minister to him through the word of knowledge. As I spoke to him from the Lord, I heard these words come out of my mouth: "And you will be anointed by God to help me preach the gospel." ("Me," meaning Mark Barclay!) This man looked very confident about the word of the Lord I was giving him, but I was wondering who he was and how he would ever help me preach. After the meeting I noticed he was invited to the preachers' room for fellowship. Jorge introduced him to me, and I began to talk with him. I learned that he spoke five languages and was the interpreter for the president of the country of Paraguay. We became great friends, and I flew him to different places to be my interpreter. We worked together for many years before he went on to be with Jesus.

Maybe someday you and I can sit down, and I could continue to tell you more supernatural stories of my Book-of-Acts-level experiences as a missionary.

In 1987, while on the mission field and casting out demons, healing the sick, and building the churches, Jesus told me to go home and deal with the American Church. He told me to strengthen the American preachers because my country will be in great moral decay and may even submit to the antichrist himself. In 1987 this seemed pretty impossible. There was abortion but not dissection of babies. There were homosexuals but not legalized gay marriage. There were user-friendly churches but not secular churches. There was a little false doctrine preached here and there but not all the heresy we hear about today. We had a few pastors with wrong motives but nowhere near this number of hirelings. Around the year 2000 I began to see clearly why the Lord sent me home. I could see why the Lord needed another prophet who would speak for Him and confront this nonsense and wrongdoing.

17

FROM WHERE HAVE ALL THESE PREACHERS COME?

Back in the 1970s when the Lord told me He would make me a general in His army, I had no idea what all that meant. I had no idea how much work that would be. I also had no idea how much weight and responsibility it would be.

It all started in 1980 when I would go to other pastors and buy them lunch and encourage them. I did not do this with any intentions of building a network of ministers. Time and again I would travel to another nearby city and visit with a pastor and take him an offering. I would be a friendly listening ear and someone with whom they could bare their heart.

After doing this for a couple of years, I actually felt the call of God to strengthen ministers and bless any minister with whom I came in contact. I just fell in love with the tenacity of ministers and the heart they have toward the gospel. Many of them were so beat up and worn out. Many were very tired or even suffered burnout, and many had that sick heart that comes from having your dream deferred (Prov. 13:12).

The more I pursued this journey to encourage ministers, the more I felt the burden. Because I was also a pastor, I could feel what they were going through and had deep compassion for them. I knew more and more that this was to be part of my call.

As this part of my ministry grew, I found myself traveling farther away in a larger circumference. Many times I would drive most of the day, just to sit down with a pastor and have him tell me his vision and share his heart with me. I learned quickly that most ministers are alone, or at least feel alone, and they trust very few people (if anyone) with their private life. This hurt my heart. I have always had a father in the faith and a pastor. I have always had a man of God to whom I could turn.

The Lord began to groom me to be a leader among leaders. I knew deep inside that I was to spend more and more time ministering to the fivefold ministry gifts. As I obeyed God in this, more and more ministers hooked up with me. The word began to spread from one minister to another that there was a man named Barclay who would help them and pray over them and understood what they were going through.

Everywhere I went, ministers of the gospel were drawn to me and still are today. Even in other countries they would ask me to hold special meetings for ministers or at least spend a few minutes with them individually. I even started writing things that would fortify them. I began to sign my letters with "DON'T QUIT!" I started and closed many of our recordings with "DON'T QUIT!" Countless times I have thanked ministers for not quitting.

Today, hundreds and hundreds of ministers call me general, father, pastor, mentor, bishop, or apostle. I have never asked anyone to call me by these titles. I'm not trying to build my own kingdom or recruit anyone. I simply have a heart to help and a call to do so.

I have written books just for preachers. I hold private meetings for preachers, called Live Straight Talk for Ministers. I have a three-year video school (Supernatural Ministries Training Institute) designed to equip their helpers and build people around them. The school specializes in helps and practicalities and building a great team around church leaders. The school, available in English, French, and Spanish, has graduated thousands of students and operates in several different countries.

I always have preachers around me. Almost every day of my life I have a fivefold minister with me to sit in a service or meet with me. One man said, "Brother Barclay, you are like a magnet, and ministers are just drawn to you."

Vickie and I spend most of our lives now pouring into ministers of the gospel. We spend hours daily on the telephone with these great gospel leaders. We also have ministers constantly visiting us at Living Word International Church in Midland, Michigan. Seldom do we have church without a guest minister coming to sit in the service. Often they bring their team to observe ours and expose them to the level of cooperation we have here at the home church. Pastors frequently send their key helps people to spend time with ours. We consider it a high privilege to be able to inspire others and share anything and everything we have to build local churches around the world.

Many have told me that as they travel from church to church and visit with the pastors, my name is brought up as one who has inspired them and probably even ministered to them personally at one time or another. Though we love all believers, Vickie and I have been assigned by the Head of the Church to be like a mom and dad to those who stand at the holy desk, no matter their office in the fivefold.

We certainly do not claim to know it all, but what we do know, we want to share. I am not of the school that says, "I learned it the hard way, and so can you." I believe that whatever we have learned among many witnesses we are to pass on to faithful brothers and sisters who will teach others also.

In this book I've shared my heart for my fathers in the faith. I constantly quote them. I recently heard a young preacher say, "We need to stop using the names of these old preachers who have gone to Heaven because no one even knows who they are anymore." My response to him was simple: "The reason they do not know is because you have been dishonorable and have not given credit where credit is due nor honor where honor is due. What if those before us had done the same regarding Peter, James, John, and so on?"

For a long time I was so busy working at being a good son to my fathers in the faith that I didn't realize God was grooming *me* to be a father in the faith. My fathers are now all in Heaven. I thank God for the investment they made in my life. Anytime I have an opportunity to give them credit, I shall do it. This isn't anything they ever asked me to do, and of course I have never asked any man to do this toward me.

In my personal prayer area I have a picture of each one of these "Greats." I also have a hallway just outside of my prayer room called the Hall of Faith. I have a picture of each one of these fathers in my pulpit. On my pulpit is a plaque that has their names listed. It reminds me where I came from, whom God used to grow me up, and who stood by my side during that process. I can constantly hear my pastor, John Osteen, say, "Mark, if you forget where you came from, you'll never get where you're supposed to go."

Every day of my life now I have another minister ask me, "Can you give me some time? Can I be part of your life? Can you advise me? Is there any way I can look to you as a leader? Can you be my pastor?" And though I am only one man, I always say, "Yes, I will help you in any way I possibly can."

For this reason I started a ministerial network several years ago called the Righteous Preachers' Network. I formed a team of gospel leaders and called them the President's Cabinet. They have helped me tremendously in my national and international efforts. These men have also been a great strength to help me minister to ministers. They all feel led to help others become connected to this level of fellowship, where there is no big guy or little guy and it isn't based on how big your church or ministry is. There are presently only a few hundred ministers in our fellowship, but I know in my heart it will climb to the thousands. I'm not trying to do this. It is not my goal to grow an army of followers. It is my goal to help as many ministers of the gospel as I possibly can, with every means available to me by God.

There is no reason why any fivefold minister must be alone. There is no good reason why he or she has to relate to a picture on a wall or a Bible school certificate, realizing they rarely have any communication at all with that leader anymore. I hear from ministers from every continent on the globe. I consider it a high honor to call them, text them, e-mail them, and share whatever wisdom and anointing I have.

I remember the day the Lord told me to start Supernatural Ministries Training Institute. I sat alone, day after day, writing the curriculum. I had these ministers on my mind. I kept asking the Lord how I could train the soldiers of the cross to be great disciples, find their own ministry, and help their pastors build a powerful, supernatural local church. Every class outline (hundreds of them) was written by my own hand as I spent time before God with this on my mind.

I remember when the Lord told me to start making recordings for ministers. I call that Straight Talk for Ministers and mail it to them free of charge. It began with just a handful of ministries, and now I'm giving it to hundreds of gospel ministers around the world.

I remember when the Lord told me to start holding private ministers' meetings, which we call Live Straight Talk for Ministers. We do a few of these every year. I invite ministers to come for two days to get in a closed room with Vickie and me, where I share my heart, deal with the pertinent matters of the day, and give them time to ask questions. We always receive communion together, and I anoint every one of them with oil and the laying on of hands. Ministers who have attended from around the world tell me that it's one of the most life-changing things they've ever done.

I remember when the Lord told me to put together a ministry of helps manual that pastors and church leaders could use to train their teams. Whether you are a small church or a large one, we all require the same supportive ministry departments and people who are trained, qualified, and willing to help bear that responsibility. All churches will eventually need greeters, ushers, an audio team, a worship team, a nursery, children's church workers, and so on.

I remember the day the Lord told me to write a practicalities manual called *Minister's Manual* that pastors can use for themselves and to train their helps leaders and future ministers. In this manual I cover many facets of ministry—visitation, baptisms, child dedication, funerals for sinners, funerals for Christians, weddings, how to build leaders around you, what to do when trouble comes, etc.

I remember the day the Lord told me to write a book on how to relate to your pastor because so many people were coming out of so many different denominations where they had different church governments and maybe even different views about the role of the pastor. I first called it *Seven Bible Ways to Properly Relate to Your Pastor* because I used seven major New Testament verses to show the body of Christ what a strength this would bring to their lives. This little book is going around the world, and I personally know for a fact that hundreds of pastors have used it to bring understanding to the people around them. My pastor, John Osteen, told me that God has used me to restore honor back to the office of the pastor.

Since then I have written dozens of books to help the body of Christ fit into this wonderful kingdom of God and the local church, which is the training center and the place of the altar for all believers.

My son Josh was traveling with me one time as part of our ministry team. In a Sunday morning service we preached in a church with several thousand people. On that same day we flew three states away where I preached in an evening service to a congregation of about 20 people. After that evening service Josh said to me, "Dad, you're a very unusual leader, that you would even come to such a small place in the middle of nowhere for just twenty-some people." I told him I have no problem speaking to a smaller group of believers because they also deserve the same Word and the same anointing as a large congregation does. I explained that we are sent to minister to everyone. I preached that evening to stand with that man, that fivefold ministry gift who calls me his pastor. I told Josh I wanted that pastor to know that I am standing with him. I wanted the angels to notice. I wanted the demons to know. I wanted every one of those believers to know. And now they have living proof that it is so.

I believe it is extremely important that, as a leader, I stand with those who are looking up to me and those who have submitted to the authority and the seniority on my life. I'm not sure I have perfected being a father in the faith yet, but I'm giving it my best shot. I realize I am only one man and can't get to every minister's church everywhere. But I can stand with them in faith and touch as many as I possibly can.

From where have all these preachers come? They are sent from the Lord so believers can have a leader in their life and a voice of strength and anointing. Please pray for Vickie and me!

18

BOOKS, BOOKS, AND MORE BOOKS

I HAVE WRITTEN MANY BOOKS FOR GOD'S PEOPLE

When I was in high school, I was totally dislocated from life. I was a very confused young man. When it came to academics, I was a horrible student. I must admit that I really didn't have any desire to study, but I would study just enough to pass tests and then go on to the next grade.

I was so angry and filled with hate that mostly all I did was fight and cause issues for teachers and other students. It was no surprise to me that I was kicked out of school and told to never come back.

When I enlisted in the Marine Corps, I went to the Army and Navy Academy in Carlsbad, California, and earned my high school diploma. It actually felt pretty good to get that diploma in my hand when I had been told all my young life that I would never graduate and never amount to anything. I was so proud to send that diploma to my mom.

I didn't realize that to be in the U.S. Marines you had to go to classes and learn things… and learn them quickly! I found out right away that we were not there just to shoot guns and practice drills. All those classes began to change me, and for the first time I began to realize that I was not just a dummy and a loser.

Though I was far from being a clerk or doing administrative work for the Corps, I began to write things down and kept a pretty thorough record of all that I did. I realize now that keeping all those reports and records was God training me and preparing me to later write for Him.

Well, "later" came. It was a typical winter day in Michigan. I was sitting in my office, looking out the window at the sun glistening off the fresh snow that had fallen the night before, when the Lord spoke to me and instructed me to write my very first book. I remember saying to Him, "Me? Write a book? Are You crazy?"

As I sat in that little office, God began to speak to me about writing down the truths I had learned and sharing them. I was in the pastorate now, but my only experience as an author was writing a small dissertation for one of my degrees from Bible college. I felt overwhelmed with this assignment. Even so, I began to write. I felt the anointing of God come upon me to write. I finished that book and haven't set my pen down since. I have written dozens of books for the body of Christ and have become a popular author for other ministry magazines and periodicals. I actually wrote all three years of curriculum for our Bible college, Supernatural Ministries Training Institute (SMTI).

Following is a list of some of the most frequently requested books I have written up to this point:

Ministry of Helps Manual

Minister's Manual

How to Relate to Your Pastor

The Missing Red Letters

Avoiding the Pitfalls of Familiarity

How to Survive a Betrayal

Walking With God

The Real Truth About Tithing

The Remnant Church

Things You Need for the Day Ahead

Beware of Seducing Spirits

Sheep, Goats, and Wolves

I also ended up starting our own publications department, where I not only publish our books but also the *Preacher of Righteousness* magazine.

As I wrote the books, I used to ask the Lord if anyone would ever actually read them. I have now seen my books everywhere we go. I have enjoyed seeing my books and our SMTI curriculum translated in different languages. Many churches around the world use my books in their membership classes, and many Bible schools offer them as part of their curriculum. I see them online, in bookstores, and even on other traveling ministers' product tables.

I remember being in a remote area on the mission field, and as the people gathered for our meeting, I noticed they were standing in a group, swapping papers. As I approached them out of curiosity, they told me they were trading pages of a book. They said that because they only had one of these books, they took it apart and shared the pages and passed them around so they could all eventually read the entire book. It was *my* book, *Seven Bible Ways to Properly Relate to Your Pastor.*

I was in Singapore speaking at a convention on my way to New Zealand and Australia. A man came up to me and introduced himself as a missionary to Muslim countries and said he had just returned from being in the desert. I asked him where he had been and what he had been doing there. I also asked him what he was doing in Singapore. He said the Lord had spoken to him that the person who wrote the book he had been speaking from was going to be there in Singapore. He then held up one of my books and said he had been speaking from this book to the Muslim people. The book was pretty ragged looking and very worn. When I saw it, the Lord reminded me of what He had promised—that if I would write the books, He would distribute them, and people all over the world would read them. I told this man (who actually ended up being a good friend) that I would not only give him a new book but many others to give away as he traveled. I also laid hands on him and anointed him with oil. Then I spoke directives to him through the prophet's mantle on my life. He told me years later that those few minutes in Singapore literally changed his life forever. Isn't the Lord good!

The Lord has kept His word, and I have kept mine. I'm not sure why the Lord wanted me to be an author, but He surely did, and He continues to lead me about what to write. God has helped me write almost 40 books to date, curricula, magazines, and more. Think about it… a high school dropout, filled with hatred and rage, and then… Jesus Christ!

It just reminds me again and again that this isn't about you and me; it's about obeying Him. I am not a half-full cup. To say it in the King James language, I am not a cup that tippeth over; I'm a cup that "runneth" over. I am not a partially purchased vessel. I am a vessel full of God. I am God possessed! And I will write on.

19

ME? PASTOR?
GOD HELP US ALL!

It was 1979. I had just resigned as youth pastor at the church we were assigned to at the time. I was traveling some, and between meetings I was teaching at Berean Bible College in San Diego. Every morning I would go to the college chapel and pray with all the students. I would crawl under a pew and spend every moment with God I possibly could. There, under that pew, is where I learned to hear from God. I also turned our bedroom closet in our apartment into an actual prayer closet.

As I was under that pew at Berean Bible College, I saw a vision. It was so real. I could see it with my eyes open and closed. I felt the authority of God all over me. At the time all I could compare it to was the beginning frames of a television program I watched as a kid, a western called Bonanza. At the beginning of this program, there was a scene of the Ponderosa Ranch on a map, and a spark began, and then a flame, and then it consumed the map. This vision reminded me of that scene on that program.

The map in my vision was the state of Michigan. The spark (almost like a sparkler) started in the center of the state. It consumed the state and then the vision was over, but it so consumed me that I went home and prayed over it for the longest time. I knew there was a deep, godly reason I saw this vision.

On another day after that, I was under the same pew, in the same chapel, when I saw the vision again. It was almost identical to what I had seen before. I could see this vision, whether my eyes were open or shut. It was an open vision. It started with that same spark, in the same spot, and began to spread flames across Michigan, only this time it spread throughout the Great Lakes Region. I was so consumed by it I had to go home and pray and meditate in it. What was the Lord Jesus trying to say to me?

And, believe it or not, it happened a third time—same chapel, same pew, same vision, only this time the flames spread across the entire country and beyond. The power of God hit me so hard it was as though I was paralyzed. I cried out to the Lord and asked Him what He wanted from me.

Then the Lord spoke clearly to me: "Where the spark begins, I want you to build Me an army and a headquarters. Make your plans now, and move when I tell you."

I noticed that all the other students had gone from their time of prayer, but I was still there. When I arrived home, I grabbed Vickie by the hand, ran for my atlas, and threw it on the bed. I began to tell her for the first time about these three visions I had. Up to this point, I had shared them with no one. When I opened that map of the United States and looked at the state of Michigan, I put my finger perfectly where I had seen the sparks start all three times. It was in Midland, Michigan!

I had only been there one other time, as a teenager. I knew no one there. But I knew that I knew that I knew that God was telling me to go there. When I showed Vickie and told her what God had said, she said, "No way. I doubt that is God." As we talked about it, she seemed to be more and more reluctant and couldn't figure out why on this earth the Lord would move us from San Diego (just when things were finally going well for us) back to the state of Michigan to a city where we knew nobody.

I began to pray and sometimes wrestled with this into the night. As I spoke to God, I would tell Him, "You're going to have to tell this to Vickie Yourself in order for her to know this is You and follow." I just got to the point where I would not discuss it with her anymore. And then one night, deep into the night, I was awakened by Vickie, shaking me and saying, "The Lord wants us to move to Midland, Michigan, the very city where the beginning of that flame started. We must obey God." "Yes, dear," I said, and lay there a few minutes before I fell back to sleep, thanking the Lord for His guidance and leadership in our life.

We had literally no idea all that was in store for us as we prayed about making this move. I did know enough to pray, so on every Tuesday night after a day of fasting, Vickie and I and some of our friends and partners met together at my house, and we prayed about this entire vision.

As the vision became more clear and the timing approached, we had a much better picture of what the Lord had for us. "Build an army!" the Lord said. "I will bring people to help you, and they will never stop coming. If Midland doesn't receive you, I will bring people to you from other places to be a part of your army. You will have to pastor them and watch over their soul, but you will not build a typical local church. You will build an army of believers who will help you reach the unreached and tell the untold."

It is to the miracle power of God and His glory how all this came together and how we even had the money to make the move. But in the spring of 1980, we started Living Word International Outreach Center in Midland, Michigan. It would take volumes to tell you all the miracles that took place and how the church began to grow. Those first believers were so awesome. Many of them are still with me all these years later, including Lori Lang (her husband Craig came later), Gary and Susan

Smith, Randy and Diane Saylor, Kim and Robin Livesay, Roger and Diane Ellison, and many others.

We have always used the illustration of David in the cave of Adullam, where he ran to hide and a multitude of men gathered unto him. The Scriptures tell us that it was everyone in debt, distressed, and discontented; and he became a captain over them. This is exactly what has happened here in Midland, Michigan. Many people have submitted themselves to the things of God and have come and gathered to me, and we have built a great army. However, I had to *become* a captain over them. I finally had to admit that God has gifted me to not only lead His people but to feed them. That gift to pastor would become an integral part of my entire life and ministry.

From this very location (where I saw the spark in the vision), all these many years later, things have grown and unfolded, just like the Lord said. We are no longer just a handful. The church is hundreds strong, and ministers from around the world are coming and going from here. We have our own publications department. We have our own Bible training center. We shoot the national telecast right from this location. And it is no longer the cave at Adullam, rather my world headquarters.

There is seldom a church service at Living Word when a minister and his family are not joining us to ask me for the wisdom of God and to pray over their life and ministry. Though I spend the majority of my time in my own country now, the United States of America, hoping to save and protect the Bible and the United States Constitution, I am still absolutely a global missionary, and we are an international operation.

Vickie and I now find ourselves pastoring multitudes of pastors and ministers from around the world. Many call us apostle, bishop, father in the faith, mentor, mom and dad, grandma and grandpa, and yes, even pastor—just like the Lord said back in that prayer closet in 1979!

If you are ever able to visit or attend Living Word you will be blessed, and we will be blessed to have you.

20

THE MIGHTY ARMY OF HELPS

In 1979, when the Lord told me to move to Central Michigan and build an army for Him and that He would cause us to reach the world from there, I asked Him how I would ever do that. He promised to send me men and women who would serve with me (many of them for a lifetime) and that all I had to do was teach them and train them, just like I learned to do as a Marine instructor. He showed me how to build a team for Him and how to function as an army—the army of God.

So, in the spring of 1980, we started holding services, and just like the Lord promised, people began to come. One of the first couples was Gary and Susan Smith. I had no idea that day they would turn out to be among my closest friends in life and ministry. Gary and Susan received the gifting of the ministry of helps (the gift that God put in them by the laying on of hands), and as I drew it out of them, it became one of the most powerful elements of our ministry. Here we are, decades later, and Gary is still leading the mighty army of helps and continues to train the young ones. I have always said that Gary Smith could motivate a dead mule. Whether it is a remodel job, yard detail, painting, ushering, or hosting a conference, somehow Smitty always makes it exciting and fun to serve.

I have always believed that every Christian is called by God, not just the preachers. Every man and woman is gifted to help build the house of God. We all have a part. We are all members in particular. You are as "called" as your pastor. You will give the same account to Jesus for your ministry as I will for mine. Smitty and I have proven that a local church is the greatest place to discover your call and learn to walk in it, and there is nothing more satisfying and fulfilling than serving the King of Glory with the gift He gave you.

And speaking of lifelong friends, soon after the Smiths came Kim and Robin Livesay. Kim became our head deacon and helped build a powerful deacons' and ushers' team that grew into one of the best in the ministry. Kim and Robin are still with us today. They are a gold mine as well. They have never quit. They have been a key element in the ministry of helps here at Living Word.

Another couple who turned out to be a valuable asset is Randy and Diane Saylor. Randy not only grew under my ministry and helped grow my ministry, but he became a powerful flock care minister and assistant to me. Our church would not be what it is without them. They have been such a strength to my family, but they have also helped our members to be the best Christians they can be. Without them serving in the ministry with me all these years, Living Word Church and Mark Barclay Ministries would be much weaker and only a fraction of its size.

Lori Lang hooked up with us in California in one of our meetings there. She ended up moving to Midland and grew up in the ministry as one of our daughters. Lori helped our church build one of the greatest children's ministries in the Kingdom. She married a great young man in our church (our worship leader, Craig), and they are still with us today. Together with their family they have been a tremendous asset, blessing, and gift to our church for many years.

I remember the day Roger and Diane Ellison came into my life and into our church. Roger was involved in Full Gospel Business Men's Fellowship International, where I actually met him when I was a speaker at one of their events. Soon after, he and Diane showed up at one of our church services and began to attend regularly. Just before the service one morning, Roger approached me with a great surprise announcement. He felt led to replace my old, beat-up car with a new one! I remember him saying to me, "I can't have my pastor driving a car like this, so I'm going to give you this one, but promise me you won't give the old car you've been driving to anybody we know!" We both laughed. Roger and Diane also felt led to pay for the very first book I ever wrote. They are still with me today, and their story goes on and on.

If space would allow, I could say something about each and every person and each and every couple God sent to us and became such a great part of this army. There are just so many of them… and He is still sending more!

We have always compared Living Word International Outreach Center to the cave Adullam, where David ran to hide from Saul and the threats on his life. There, in that cave, four hundred men found him and gathered to him. Whatever happened in that cave was life changing for everyone, including David. They went from being very troubled men to becoming David's army of mighty men. (For more on this, read my book, *The Captain's Mantle.*)

1 SAMUEL 22:1-2

David therefore departed thence, and escaped to the cave Adullam: and when his brethren and all his father's house heard *it*, they went down thither to him. And every one *that was* in distress, and every one that *was* in debt, and every one *that was* discontented, gathered themselves unto him; and he became a captain over them: and there were with him about four hundred men.

2 SAMUEL 23:8

These *be* the names of the mighty men whom David had…

There is no way I could fulfill my call in God and travel the world over without this great army of helpers. They will do anything… and they do. Nothing seems to be too big for them. No challenge seems to be too overwhelming. No matter what I ask them to do (and many times I don't even need to ask), they attack it as unto the Lord. They are fierce. They are fearless. They are dedicated. They are faithful. They are godly. They are anointed. They are there for me, night and day. Their fingerprints are all over my life and ministry.

They have not only helped me but many other people and other ministries as well—everything from world missions trips, to helping stand ministers back up again, to roofing someone's house. Their outreaches alone have changed our city and the people in it. They are always doing something to love on people and witness the good news of Jesus Christ. I have seen them feed the poor; feed hundreds at Thanksgiving; hand out Christmas boxes of goodies; host special events at the county fair; and provide ministry at the hospitals, convalescent homes, and even the jails. They are constantly looking after the true widows and helping those who are hurting. They have been a mighty army and have not only helped me but have brought great encouragement to Vickie and my family. This verse reminds me of them: "I beseech you, brethren, (ye know the house of Stephanas, that it is the firstfruits of Achaia, and *that* **they have addicted themselves to the ministry of the saints**…" (1 Cor. 16:15).

This army of helps has become notorious. Many people from around the world come to Living Word to see how it all functions. I could not begin to tell you the hundreds and hundreds of ministers who have come to see this team in action and brought people with them to observe this mighty army of helps in operation over the last three decades. I have testified about them, and I have done entire seminars about their ministry in an attempt to inspire God's people everywhere to serve the Lord Jesus Christ in such a way and to help their pastor build great churches. I have all kinds of teachings available on recorded media, as well as my *Ministry of Helps Manual*, books, and the entire first year of our SMTI Bible training center (Supernatural Ministries Training Institute).

I have no idea what I would do without them. A general is only as good as his troops in the field. It is so refreshing and brings hope for the future when I see so many young people digging in and serving God with all their heart. In the midst of the sea of humanity and the multitudes of young people who do not want God and don't want to serve Him, there is a mighty army of helps that will continue the work of our Lord.

Besides all that, every believer must have an avenue to serve the Lord with great gratitude and help preach the gospel of the Lord Jesus Christ. We know we can't pay Him back, but we can spend a lifetime trying and saying thank You with more than our mouth.

We all have a ministry. We all are dually gifted. We all have a gift to serve within the church family to build each other up and build great churches that help us all in our second gifting, which is to reach the unreached and tell the untold. It's called the ministry of reconciliation— winning the lost and making disciples.

2 CORINTHIANS 5:18

And all things *are* of God, who hath reconciled us to himself by Jesus Christ, and hath given to us the ministry of reconciliation…

MATTHEW 28:18-20

And Jesus came and spake unto them, saying, All power is given unto me in heaven and in earth. Go ye therefore, and teach all nations, baptizing them in the name of the Father, and of the Son, and of the Holy Ghost: Teaching them to observe all things whatsoever I have commanded you: and, lo, I am with you alway, *even* unto the end of the world. Amen.

1 CORINTHIANS 12:28

And God hath set some in the church, first apostles, secondarily prophets, thirdly teachers, after that miracles, then gifts of healings, helps, governments, diversities of tongues.

1 SAMUEL 14:7

And his armourbearer said unto him, Do all that *is* in thine heart: turn thee; behold, I *am* with thee according to thy heart.

1 SAMUEL 14:13

And Jonathan climbed up upon his hands and upon his feet, and his armourbearer after him: and they fell before Jonathan; and his armourbearer slew after him.

2 CORINTHIANS 6:1

We then, *as* workers together *with him,* beseech *you* also that ye receive not the grace of God in vain.

21

THE FIRST FAMILY

First of all, Vickie and I did not come up with the name "First Family." We have always seen ourselves as one of the many families that have paid a dear price to be a part of this team and build such a powerful, stable, and anointed church family. It was others around us who wanted to honor and take care of us and started referring to us as the First Family.

The First Family of Living Word International Church and Mark Barclay Ministries began back in the 1970s with Vickie's mom, Shirley St. Dennis. She was the one who began to take us to church and prayer meetings. I met Vickie at age 13, and as far back as I can remember, Mama Shirley wanted to be around us kids. We were used to that. When we all started serving God, she would serve with us. She was one of the very first people to tell me that she believed I was called by God to be a preacher and that God would use my voice in the very end of times. She always believed that I would be one of those who would actually prepare the body of Christ for His coming. Shirley moved back to Michigan with us when we made the journey to start our world headquarters, and until the day she was promoted to Heaven she served here with all her might.

Vickie has always been a leader among women and sets a powerful example for them to follow, whether young or older. This leadership really showed up in her when she was a Marine wife, and especially when I was deployed to Vietnam twice. She has been right there by my side, and without her we would certainly be limping along today instead of running full speed ahead. She is an excellent speaker and is also traveling, fulfilling her own ministry in the pulpits of God. She has a great message from "Mom" to the congregations, as well as a powerful testimony about Jesus healing her from cancer. Many pastors and ministers say that Vickie Barclay is the happiest person they know.

My daughter Dawn was born in 1972. I was still in Vietnam. Vickie had to tackle that by herself. I wanted to be there with all my heart, but it just wasn't going to happen. Thank God I was one of those who made it home from the war and had the awesome privilege of raising up my children in the way they should go.

Dawn grew up to be a great lady. Her mama taught her how to be a woman and a woman of God. She now has a great husband, James, and four wonderful children. She has proven to be a powerful wife as well as a powerful mom. She is very well educated in the Scriptures and lives by these wonderful truths. She is highly respected by those who know her. She is a no-compromise person and stands on God's Word, no matter what. I am so proud of her and the life she has chosen to live.

Dawn has been a leader in God's house since she was a young lady. She is a great Bible teacher and does an awesome job in the pulpit. She has always had her hand on our children's ministries, youth, and young adults. She has helped raise up many other believers who are now serving in our church as adults.

Dawn is also a favorite conference speaker and stays busy in our own church as well as traveling to help others. Her ability to communicate and organize has helped her strengthen many others in all walks of life.

My dear friend, Senator Rick Santorum, even asked her to help during his campaign for President of the United States.

I still remember the day Dawn talked to me about a new member of our church, a young man, James Randolph. She presented him to me as if he were a prince on a white horse! He had completed SMTI (our Bible school), and he was a born-again, water-baptized, Spirit-filled Christian. She also threw in there that he was handsome and that she was very attracted to him. Well, after working out a couple things with God (and quite a few things with Dad ☺), she and James started courting.

It turned out that James truly was and is a very severe man of God. He is a man of the Bible and lives in it. He is a great dad and husband. Our church loves him. He is so gifted that he could pastor a church anywhere, but he chooses to help me. He is technically my son-in-law, but Vickie and I say he is our son as though we birthed and raised him ourselves. Like me, he has a powerful testimony of God's grace and delivering power—once a very messed-up and sin-filled youth who since received a powerful and dynamic deliverance and promotion in the Kingdom. James helps a lot of people with his gift to exhort, his knowledge of the Scriptures, and his ability to relate to people. Many times our staff and family say, "Ask James… he knows everyone in the whole city!"

My son Josh was born in 1976. We were going to Bible college in California at the time. There were complications with his birth (I explained this in more detail in another chapter), and it was truly a divine miracle that he was born healthy and whole and that his mama was okay as well. I clearly remember the day that God spoke to me and told me I would have a son, and to name him Joshua, and that he would help me preach the gospel to the world all of my life. I remember telling Vickie that if she would just get him out of the diaper stage, I would take him with me every day. She did, and I did. Josh has been at my side as far back as he can remember. He has traveled all over the world with me. He now travels on his own as God has anointed him in his own right to preach the gospel and to work the holy altars.

Josh has always been known as one who quotes the phrase, "Whatever it takes!" It is one of the principles he lives by. Like me, he seldom takes no as a final answer.

Josh has grown up to be a great man of God. He is shaking his world and his generation. He is very well received and also respected and looked up to by the generation that is coming up under him. He is and will continue to be a powerful rescuing voice and one God uses to climax the ages.

I remember the day that God first supernaturally connected Josh and his beautiful wife Trish. We were preaching for one of my sons in the faith, James P. Crabb, in Cincinnati. I had spoken for James P. many times before but for some reason Josh and Trish had never actually met. Vickie noticed immediately how they looked at each other. I thought, no way! Josh has spent his whole life up to now teasing his sister with blonde jokes and persecuting Buckeyes. I used to tell him, "Josh, just keep it up, and one day you will marry a blonde Buckeye." Well, that night at Courts of Praise Church in Hamilton, Ohio, she came into the sanctuary, a blonde Buckeye.

Trish is a godsend to us. I have watched how she takes care of my son Josh and how she raises her babies. She is not only a God-chosen, perfect fit for Josh, but she is a perfect fit for a global ministry family like ours. She is one of the sharpest businesswomen I have ever met, and her gifting in this area has brought many good things to our family and our ministry. God knew before the foundations of the earth what kind of woman could live in such heavy anointing and take on the wicked persecution and slander that our ministry faces daily. Trish comes from a God-fearing family and was influenced so deeply by the Crabb family that she calls them Ma and Pa. We are very thankful that she grew up serving Jesus.

I remember when my two kids were just little infants. I would sit and rock them in the night and hold them up to God and say, "Lord Jesus, if You give me their heart, they will give You their life; but if not, they will eventually stop listening to me and will be influenced by another."

I anointed my kids with oil, long before they ever knew what I was doing. I can't tell you how many times I dedicated them to the Lord and to the service of the King of Glory. Vickie and I made an agreement that she would train up Dawn to be a woman of God and a good wife and mom, and I would raise up Josh to be a bold leader and a strong husband and man of God. Our plan worked. Sure, I was a dad to Dawn, and Vickie was a mom to Josh; but we knew what we had to impart to them.

All the years my kids were growing up, we served the Lord. We not only served the Lord at church, but we were real Christians at home. I never, ever gave my kids any reason or excuse at all for missing church, and they never asked. I used to tell them that they must either serve God, or die. What I meant by that is there are only two options in life— serve God and stay on His life cycle, or don't serve God and live on a death cycle where only bad things happen to you. After my kids grew up they told me that for a long time they thought I meant to serve God or I was going to kill them. I guess it worked both ways!

Our claim is that our grandkids and great-grandkids will always serve the Lord. Dawn and James have four children: Merceades (married to Derek), Dakota, Jadyn, and Liberty. Josh and Trish have three children: Mark Jude, Malakai, and London. All are born-again Christians. At this writing, Vickie and I also have a great-grandson, Theo.

We all live in the same city, and we all serve in the same ministry. We love each other, and we actually even *like* each other (most of the time). God has graced us to reach the world as a family, and this First Family will never do anything to frustrate that grace of God in vain.

22

THE NEXT PHASE OF MINISTRY

It was at campmeeting in Tulsa, Oklahoma—in 1985, if my memory serves me right. Dr. Hagin was speaking, and he made a statement that really set things in order for me. He said, "I am just now entering into my second phase of ministry." Phase of ministry, I thought. That explains it all. That brought definition to me and explained why things were changing in me and why these adjustments were continually being made in my life. Here I was at campmeeting, and finally things began to make better sense to me.

The first phase of my ministry was to serve in the ministry of helps. I had progressed slowly through the phases of Christianity the Lord set in the Church. All of us were first converts, then epistles, then disciples, and then ministers.

I had submitted myself to a good pastor and good training in the local church. I finished my Bible college training at L.I.F.E. Bible College and then Berean Bible College while also studying for my doctorate.

In 1979 the Lord spoke to me to reposition myself to Midland and step into the ministry of the apostle and pioneer the work there. I obeyed. But I realized when I began to walk this out that it wasn't just a new assignment. The anointing and the intensity totally changed in my life. With it came a new and different insight into His kingdom and what He expected from me.

I had already moved to Midland, Michigan, and started the ministry there. At this time the church was five years old. I was in the full swing of pastoring those beautiful believers. I had stopped itinerating while I pioneered the church; but it was time to put the pedal to the metal once again, and I resumed my traveling ministry. I was going out of the country two or three times a year, taking believers and ministers with me.

During this time the Lord also spoke to me to establish works in other countries. "Build this army in Midland, and go to the world," He said. I was taught early on that some send, some go, and some do both. God chose me to be the "both" guy. I believe that with every vision of God there is a supernatural provision. So as I prayed about world missions, God brought people to me who wanted to work with me and were willing to help fund the trips. It was such a blessing to be a part of what God was doing and to help plant churches and establish Bible schools, missions, and printing facilities all over the world. I was always going to learn a second language, but we were in so many different countries I couldn't lock down on which language to learn!

In 1985 the Lord spoke to me with a new assignment: "Warn My people of the coming spirits of the antichrist, and teach them about the day of My coming." It was amazing to me how few people wanted to hear about it. As I warned them of the day of Noah, the day of Lot, and the remnant Church, more and more people seemed to pull away from me. It just wasn't what our liberal society wanted to hear, and neither did the lukewarm Church. I preached it anyway! I even wrote a book called *The Remnant* and filled our magazines with end-time insights.

In 1987 I was on the mission field preaching when the Lord said to me, "Go home to America and spend most of your speaking time there. America will become very polluted, and the Church unholy. America will make laws against My Word in unprecedented manner as she drifts to the time of the judges." I didn't understand all of that assignment when I received it. I just obeyed like a good soldier. By the mid-1990s I began to see clearly, and by the 2000s it was crystal clear. Even then parts of the Church were approving an unholy lifestyle and sexual perversion in their ranks.

In 1990 the Lord refreshed my assignment and told me to emphasize the teachings of His coming. He told me that many would begin to deny the rapture teaching and even purpose to be a foolish virgin, and they would run out of oil and their lamps would go out.

The Lord began to show me there would be a spiritual outpouring that would spawn a revival in the Church, which would spawn an outpouring to the world. He is coming for a glorious Church, without spot or blemish, no wrinkle, or any such thing. This brings me encouragement, as I know we are not there now. Much of the Church is dirty, and even filthy dirty, and I'm sad to say that many want it this way and believe the Lord doesn't care. There must be a great cleansing, a revival at the altars, and a call to repentance in order for the Church to be ready for His coming. In fact, I predict that a great part of the true Church's future will be a revival of repentance and altars filled with people desperately crying out to God.

In 1994 God spoke to me to lead His people through these times. He told me to ask pastors everywhere to open the altars again and even invite God's people to spend time there worshipping, praying, and for the laying on of hands. The altar was and is where God changes lives like nowhere else.

In 1998 the Lord adjusted my assignment again. He told me to warn His people about the coming deception related to the year 2000. Many people actually prepared for the end of the world. I told everyone that I could see that the Lord was *not* coming at the turn of the century, and the world was *not* coming to an end at that time. Fear gripped many. Billions of dollars were spent by companies worried about the clock on their computers, and people everywhere (including many Christians) stored up food and survival items enough to support a multitude. Few listened to me.

In 2007 the Lord visited me and made another adjustment in my ministry when He told me to prepare His people for His coming—not the second coming but that meeting with Him in the air (1 Thess. 4:17)—and to take a move of the Spirit to the last-days generations.

For many years I have taught about the Holy Spirit, but in obedience to this assignment I held Holy Spirit conferences all over the country and even in other countries. I have seen the great Holy Spirit manifest time and time again. Through the years, at one time or another, I have witnessed all nine gifts of the Spirit flow through me. What a tremendous blessing and high privilege to be used by the Lord, especially in these days.

In 2010 the Lord Jesus told me to give myself totally to the prophet's ministry and anointing, and He would also allow me to walk in the office of the apostle so I would be able to help many other ministers of the gospel and churches globally.

In 2012 God told me to declare "status confessionis" and boldly confront heresy and immorality.

I am sure the Lord is not done directing my path or clarifying my call. I am open and willing to obey all His commands. I report for duty every day, and as my eyes open, I say to Him, "I am Your soldier, and I am Yours to command!"

ONE EXAMPLE OF THE POWER OF THE OFFICE OF THE PROPHET

In August of 2006 I was speaking for a dear friend, Dr. Larry Gordon, and Cornerstone World Outreach in Sioux City, Iowa. As I was speaking, the Lord revealed a demon to me that was sitting on a throne with a death grip on that city and that had been responsible for hindering and harassing churches as well as agitating the economy and spiritual climate of the city. I remember telling the church that 121 years ago something happened in Sioux City and to find out what it was and do something about it.

That night Rev. Cary Gordon did some research and found that exactly 121 years before, a bold, holy, sin-confronting preacher named Haddock was shot and killed in the street for his preaching, and the murderer was not dealt with justly. At that very moment this demon took a supernatural seat of authority, and to that day it sat on that throne, ruling the city. It was dethroned that night, but the curse on the city still had to be dealt with.

Cary took on the challenge of not only researching all this but also the long and hard fight to find the truth… and he did. On August 3, 2016, I flew to Sioux City to witness and participate in a ceremony and a repentance service for the murderous crime against this preacher and the wrongdoing by the leaders of the city and the region of that day in how they dealt with this crime with great injustice. A beautiful monument of Rev. Haddock was erected in the perfect spot in the center of the city. That demon and the curse it imposed on the area is now totally broken. At that ceremony I spoke to all who were present that it would be just the beginning as other villages, towns, and cities would also find such deep-rooted injustices and make things right in the eyes of the Lord.

Many people around the world have sent in their testimonies of how a prophetic word or insight changed their life and ministry forever. Thank God for His mighty gifts and callings!

I remember one time when I was ministering to a pastor, and the Lord revealed that a very close, key person on his staff was going to turn on him and try to destroy his church and ministry. The pastor was reluctant to receive it and, in fact, I'm not sure he really did. But several months later the very man I pointed out to him did exactly what the Lord said he would do, and the church barely survived it. That pastor was so convinced that this man would never, ever do him wrong that he rejected the word of the Lord that came through the mouth of the prophet of God and almost didn't survive it.

Many government leaders and those running for office contact me and ask me about what I see through the eyes of the prophet. Many listen… many don't. Many actually quote what I tell them, or they at least turn their ship in the direction God showed me for them.

I remember ministering to a man who was the president of an African nation. I was there doing a preaching and evangelism crusade when he summoned me to his office. I went, and when I was in his presence the Lord spoke to me about him and what was coming next. Twenty years later a young man contacted me to ask if I would meet with him. He happened to be that president's son. While ministering to him and visiting together, he told me the coolest story. He explained that when I was with his dad that day so many years before, he was just a kid but was in the room. He reminded me how friendly I was to him and how I tapped him on the head and declared that his future was bright but not without struggles and heavy decisions. I sort of remembered him and all of that, but he truly did… and quite clearly.

"I have come for that blessing again," he said. He shared with me how his country was going to make him the next president and that he would not accept it without the blessing of the prophet of God. He flew all the way to America to meet with me. It is not a coincidence that I was there when he was a child and that I had a small utterance over him as I met with his dad. It was no coincidence this day that he was coming to me to receive from the Lord. He also told me that everything God spoke through me to his dad that day had come to pass, including a dream his dad had about his son becoming the president one day.

I am waiting for the Lord to command me into the future and use me however He sees fit. I know that part of my duties will be to prepare His people for His coming and the end of the age. So be it, Lord Jesus!

A WORD TO YOU

Stop right now and find a place to kneel down and ask the Lord Jesus what He has for you. What are your assignments? What is for now, and what is next? You don't always get all the directions at once, but if you create the habit of submitting to Him daily and doing your best to listen to Him, it will come clearly—phase after phase, from faith to faith, and from glory to glory.

23

40 YEARS OF MARK T. BARCLAY SECRETS

Secret #1

WORSHIP—THE SECRET PLACE

One of the greatest secrets I have learned is to tap into the anointing that is present in true worship. It can actually lead you to those precious moments called the secret place, where you find yourself directly before the Lord, alone and intimate.

> **PSALM 150:6**
>
> Let every thing that hath breath praise the Lord.
> Praise ye the Lord.

Praise

Praise is when we honor God for what He does for us.

Worship

Worship is more intimate. It is embracing Him for who He is.

ACTS 3:1-10

This man went into the temple shouting and dancing and rejoicing.

2 KINGS 3:15

The anointing on true worship enhances and calls for the prophet's office.

1 SAMUEL 16:23

Saul and David: The anointed minstrel brings great peace, even to troubled people.

Worship Techniques That Are Scriptural

ACTS 3:1-10

POSTURE IN WORSHIP

Clapping hands   (~5 scriptures)

Raising hands   (1 scripture)

Bowing   (~34 scriptures)

Kneeling   (~19 scriptures)

Sitting   (~2 scriptures)

Standing   (~42 scriptures)

Dancing   (~37 scriptures)

Skipping, leaping   (27 scriptures)

Rejoicing (agallao)   (10 scriptures)

Secret #2

GOD'S HOUSE

I have been in full attendance in God's house since the first day I learned about it. It has brought such strength to my family and me. I remember the day that I was asked for one of the greatest secrets of my life, and I said I went to church and allowed no one to run me off. There are so many beautiful things in God's house that cannot be found anywhere else. I recommend consistent church attendance to everyone everywhere. It is one of the great wells of life.

1. Anointing (the Lord) is there
2. Booster shot for spiritual immune system
3. Attitude adjustment
4. Focus adjustment
5. Decontamination station
6. Heal your situation
7. Fellowship

   PSALM 122:1

   I was glad when they said unto me, Let us go into the house of the LORD.

   PSALM 48:2

   Beautiful for situation, the joy of the whole earth, *is* mount Zion, *on* the sides of the north, the city of the great King.

   REVELATION 1:10-18

   • In the Spirit on the Lord's day

   PSALM 23:4-6

   • To dwell in the house of the Lord forever

PSALM 27:4

One *thing* have I desired of the LORD, that will I seek after; that I may dwell in the house of the LORD all the days of my life, to behold the beauty of the LORD, and to enquire in his temple.

PSALM 27:5

• In the time of trouble

1 CORINTHIANS 16:15

• Addicted to the ministry of the saints

PSALM 92:13-14

• In old age

Secret #3

GOD'S WORD

Many years ago, as a baby Christian, I quickly learned that God's Word is everything! It is the roadmap to all life. It is the Manufacturer and Creator's operational manual for the human. If we follow it completely and thoroughly, it addresses every area of life. There is a way to live the high life and not the low life. I always do what it takes to live in the Word of God and have charted my life accordingly. It has done nothing but bless me, my family, and my ministry.

My Theme Verses:

PSALM 1:1-3

PROVERBS 6:20-23

v. 21   Bind them continually.

v. 22   Goest – It shall lead thee.
Sleepest – It shall keep thee.
Awakest – It shall talk with thee.

JEREMIAH 15:16

• Thy Word was found.

NUMBERS 22:9-21

• I cannot go beyond the Word.

JOSHUA 1:8-9

• Meditate day and night.

2 TIMOTHY 3:16-17

• Word is profitable.

1. Listen to it – preaching
2. Read it – study
3. Hide it in your heart – meditation
4. Life to you
5. Health to your body

Secret #4

TITHING

Tithing is one of the greatest principles God ever established for mankind. We see in the garden of Eden that God told Adam and Eve they could have the whole garden but not to touch His tree or they would surely die. Tithing is one of the ways to prove that we are honorable sons and daughters by honoring God with the firstfruits of all of our increase, according to the Scriptures. Tithing is New Testament (Heb. 7:5) as well as Old Testament. However, we see Abraham tithing before Moses was ever born, so we know that it's not just part of the law. When my wife Vickie fought cancer, we called upon the God of the tithe to rebuke it, according to Malachi 3. He did! When my daughter-in-law Trish was diagnosed with cancer, we asked the God of the tithe to rebuke the devourer. He did!

When my granddaughter Jadyn drowned in our pool, we called upon the God of the tithe to rebuke death. He did, and she was raised from the dead.

DEUTERONOMY 14:23

- I had to learn to fear the Lord.

ZECHARIAH 14:16-17

- No worship, no rain.

HEBREWS 7:5

- Tithing is New Testament and belongs to the seed of Abraham.

LEVITICUS 27:30

- The tithe is holy unto the Lord.

- The tithe IS the Lord's and doesn't become the Lord's when we present it.

MALACHI 3:8-10

- Bring ye… The tithe is to be presented!

DEUTERONOMY 26:10

- There are two parts to the tithe—to worship Him (profession), and of course the money (the first 10 percent). If we do one and not the other, we have not tithed.

Get my book, *The Real Truth About Tithing*, and my series called "Tithers' Rights."

Secret #5

GIVING

God is so great. He is always looking out for us. He wants the best for us. He is our Father, and we are His children. There is always some kind of evil lurking in the shadows and the darkness that wants to hurt us and consume us. But God has given us a way to protect ourselves.

Many people do not realize that God created the giving system in this great Kingdom so that our tomorrows do not have to be like our yesterdays. There is a way out. You can give your way out! Many people do not realize that giving has everything to do with blocking the access of evil in your life. Check out the verses below. They have been a great blessing to my family and me. We have a whole chain of miracles where God has supernaturally rescued us and kept us.

I have always been a giver since I learned my first verse defining it. I will never stop. It has brought me out of severe poverty and rescued me many times. I am so grateful to be a Christian that my love for God and what He has done for me propels me to want to invest in telling the whole world about the great news of Jesus Christ. God so loved the world, He gave His best… and that's what I'm going to do all the days of my life. Please join me!

1. **Giving to beat evil.**

EPHESIANS 6:10-13	The evil day
2 TIMOTHY 3:1	Perilous times
1 PETER 5:5-8	Devil stalking you
ECCLESIASTES 11:1-2	Giving and evil
MALACHI 3:10-11	Rebuke the devourer and tithing
GALATIANS 6:6-8	Giving and corruption

2. **Giving to get out of debt.**

2 CORINTHIANS 9:10	Multiply seed sown

3. **Giving to change our tomorrows.**

4. **Giving because we love what the gospel has done for us.**

Secret #6

PRAYER

1. **I learned how to pray.**

   MATTHEW 6:5-7

   • I listened to how my fathers in the faith prayed.

2. **I follow the example of Jesus.**

   MATTHEW 14:23

   • He spent quiet time with the Father.

   MARK 1:35

   • He started His day with prayer.

   LUKE 6:12

   • He prayed all night long.

   MATTHEW 26:26

   • He prayed over His meals.

   LUKE 22:32

   • He prayed over His helpers.

   LUKE 22:41, 44

   • He prayed when in trouble.

3. **I start every day with prayer.**

   PROVERBS 8:17

4. **I am NEVER disconnected from the throne room.**

   1 THESSALONIANS 5:17

5. **I always have communion before me.**

   1 CORINTHIANS 11:26

6. **Prayer times are a priority (pre-service prayer, etc.)**
   ACTS 3:1

7. **I ask God about EVERYTHING before I do it, buy it, etc.**
   1 THESSALONIANS 5:16-18

8. **I FORGIVE as I pray.**
   MARK 11:25

9. **I pray in the Spirit.**
   JUDE 1:20

10. **I normally take only my Bible to prayer.**

Secret #7

I NEVER QUIT!

1. **I never stop doing good.**

   GALATIANS 6:9

   • For in due season we shall reap, if we faint not.

2. **I never surrender.**

   ACTS 20:24

   • None of these things move me.

3. **I refuse to quit.**

   MICAH 7:8

   • Don't gloat over me, my enemies.

4. **I don't lose heart.**

   2 CHRONICLES 15:7

   • When the storms of life strike, it's what happens *in* you that determines what happens *to* you.

5. **I always endure hardness.**

   2 TIMOTHY 2:3

6. **Encourage yourself in the Lord.**

   1 SAMUEL 30:6

Things to Do When You Feel Like Quitting:

- Refuse to faint (quit).

- Encourage yourself in the Lord.

- Rehearse who you are in Christ.

- Remember what you've been called to.

- Reminisce your past victories.

- Go through the motions anyway.

- Practice the presence of the Lord.

- Recordings – faith comes to build you up.

- Bible – mind washed

- Fellowship – joy and friendship

- Prayer – communing with God

- Hang around motivated believers.

Create a spiritual emergency kit. Put your prophesies, dreams, favorite verses, etc., in it. Keep it near you because when trouble comes, you don't always have time to pull all this together.

Secret #8

FREEDOM FROM PEOPLE

We live in the day of great slander. I've never seen so much disrespect in my whole life. Social sites have aided and abetted this horrible activity. Satan is the accuser of the brethren. Many years ago I asked God to deliver me from what people say about me and how they feel about me. I pay no attention to my critics unless it is my own leadership in Christ. I refuse to allow the slanderers, pukers, gossipers, and talebearers to steer my path. It's that old saying that people who love you don't care about lying gossip, and the people who care don't love you.

> **MATTHEW 5:10**
>
> Blessed *are* they which are persecuted for righteousness' sake: for theirs is the kingdom of heaven.

> **MATTHEW 5:11**
>
> Blessed are ye, when *men* shall revile you, and persecute *you*, and shall say all manner of evil against you falsely, for my sake.

> **MATTHEW 5:12**
>
> Rejoice, and be exceeding glad: for great is your reward in heaven: for so persecuted they the prophets which were before you.

> **ACTS 26:17**
>
> - Delivered from the people
> - Delivered from the Gentiles

It Is None of My Business What People Think About Me

It is my business what I think about them, especially after I learn what they think about me.

It Is None of My Business What People Say About Me

It is my business what I say about them, especially after I learn what they said about me.

They must give an account to God for their own mouth.

I am not subject to live by what they say.

I live by the words of my own mouth.

GALATIANS 1:10

- I do not live to please man.

LUKE 23:34

- I turn everyone over to God.

EPHESIANS 6:12

- I wrestle not against flesh and blood.

2 TIMOTHY 2:24

- I do not strive or debate over childish things.

2 THESSALONIANS 3:2

- I consider the source.

Secret #9

HONORABLE SON

2 TIMOTHY 2:20-21

The Bible is extremely clear that there are vessels of honor and vessels of dishonor in every great house. As you read through the Scriptures, you learn that God has no blessing for those who live a dishonorable life. I learned through the years just how much God requires us to live honorably and bring no shame to His name.

DEUTERONOMY 5:16

- If you honor your mother and father, you live a long life and it will be well with you.

PROVERBS 3:9

- Honor the Lord with thy substance and **first**fruits.

MALACHI 1:6

- Where is My honor?

ROMANS 13:7

- Honor where honor is due.

1 THESSALONIANS 5:13

- Honor your pastor.

EPHESIANS 6:2-3

Honor your parents:

- Live long
- Well with thee

1. **I am an honorable son toward God.**
   I want the Lord to be pleased with me.

2. **I honor the Lord with my money.**

3. **I am an honorable son in the faith.**
   I always wanted my fathers to be pleased with me.
   I served, saluted, and submitted to them.

4. **I have always sought to be an honorable husband.**

5. **I have always sought to be an honorable father.**

6. **I have always sought to be an honorable minister.**

Secret #10

GRATITUDE

Barclay Proverb

"Every door of life swings on the hinge of gratitude."

Staying grateful is the name of the game. It's one of the greatest secrets of my life. It has kept Vickie and me out of the gray zone and away from self-pity, discouragement, and dismay. The old hymn says to count your blessings and name them one by one… count your many blessings, and see what the Lord has done.

Every day is a gift. I tell everyone that every day is like a wet sponge. Squeeze every bit of good out of it you possibly can, even when you are down to just getting a single drop.

> **LUKE 17:11-19**
>
> 10 lepers:
>
> - One was grateful and couldn't help but give thanks.
> - All were cleansed.
> - Only one was made whole.

1. **I voice my gratitude to the Lord constantly in prayer.**
2. **I voice my gratitude to the Lord over the communion elements, which I receive just about every day.**
3. **I live for Him. I want to show Him I'm grateful.**
4. **I come to church to express my gratitude.**
5. **I serve every day in His great Kingdom to display my gratitude.**

1 CHRONICLES 29:10-14

David was full of gratitude:

1. We must praise Him.

2. Blessed the Lord in front of all.

3. He exalted the Lord.

4. Riches and honor come of Thee.

5. To make great and to make small.

6. Strength to all.

2 SAMUEL 23:13-17

- David's armorbearers – fetched water behind enemy lines.
- David poured it on the ground out of gratitude.

I am so grateful for every friend, partner, team member, and church family member who has so graciously helped me build a tremendous ministry and preach these Bible truths to a hurting, suffering, sick, and dying humanity. Their sacrifice and labor of love do not go unnoticed.

PHILIPPIANS 1:3

I thank my God upon every remembrance of you…

PHILIPPIANS 1:4

Always in every prayer of mine for you all making request with joy…

PHILIPPIANS 1:5

For your fellowship in the gospel from the first day until now…

PHILIPPIANS 1:6

Being confident of this very thing, that he which hath begun a good work in you will perform *it* until the day of Jesus Christ…

Secret #11

I WATCH THE WORDS OF MY MOUTH

MATTHEW 12:37

For by thy words thou shalt be justified, and by thy words thou shalt be condemned.

One of the greatest secrets of my life and my success is that I watch my mouth. I refuse to allow satan to use my mouth to slander or gossip. I refuse to spread death among those around me and those who hear me. I refuse to break spiritual laws and hedges with the words of my mouth.

Many times Vickie will ask me why I am so quiet, and I tell her it's because if I speak it won't be right and will bring death instead of life.

Though I learned so much from the word of faith teachers about confession, I learned about this great secret directly from the Holy Scriptures:

PROVERBS 13:2-3	Keep your mouth… keep your life.
PROVERBS 12:13-14	You will live by the fruit of your lips.
PROVERBS 15:1-4	A wholesome tongue is a tree of life.
PROVERBS 18:21	Life and death are in the power of the tongue.

Angels Respond to Biblical Words

HEBREWS 1:14

PSALM 103:20

Christians are the only sector of society and creation that puts voice to the Bible, the Word of God.

Demons Respond to Anti-Bible Words

Remember that demons are but fallen, defrocked angels, but they still respond to words of humans. It is how they are made.

- I'd rather be quiet than release demons.
- Tithing profession is so important.

   PROVERBS 26:24

   - No talebearing, gossiping, slandering, or dissembling with our lips.

   MATTHEW 12:34-37

   MATTHEW 15:11

   JAMES 3:5-8

   HEBREWS 12:15

   ROMANS 3:13

   MALACHI 3:13-14

   PROVERBS 26:20

   PROVERBS 29:11

Secret #12

I AM A FORGIVER

I have learned to forgive everyone immediately. That's right—
instant forgiveness, on the spot. That way I am free from the violator
and trespasser.

Many people think that if they don't forget, they haven't forgiven, but
actually it's just about impossible for a human to forget the violation,
especially if it adjusted their life forever. However, we can forgive.

Forgiveness doesn't mean we are healed, recovered, or restored... even
to fellowship. Forgiveness means we have dropped the charges, and we
refuse to pursue. I forgive you, but it doesn't mean I don't need some
space between us to heal. Forgiveness and trust are totally different. Just
because I forgive you doesn't mean I trust you.

Many people take grudges and unforgiveness to the grave. I refuse
to do that. Unforgiveness frees me from my violator. I don't have to
build a case against them anymore, and I don't have to tell others or
recruit a team to attack them. They are no longer in my mouth, my
mind, or my sleep.

MATTHEW 18:22-35   The unjust servant

MATTHEW 6:12   The Lord's Prayer

1. I instantly forgive.
2. I drop the charges.
3. I stop the pursuit.

4. I allow no root of bitterness.

HEBREWS 12:15
Looking diligently lest any man fail of the grace of God; lest any root of bitterness springing up trouble *you*, and thereby many be defiled…

5. I forgive when I start to pray.

MARK 11:25

Six Important Things About Forgiveness

1. Forgiveness is not based on the other person repenting!
2. Forgiveness is simply dropping the charges.
3. Forgiveness washes away the "get even" or "payback" element.
4. Forgiveness keeps the blessings flowing your way.
5. Forgiveness is not only received but given.
6. Forgiveness is given so God will forgive you.

Secret #13

THE HOLY SPIRIT

I still remember the day I was born again. I also very clearly remember the day I was filled with the Holy Ghost (baptism in the Spirit). Those were two of the greatest days of my life. I am proud to be a Spirit-filled Christian. I have, at one time or another, seen all nine gifts of the Spirit flow through me. I have literally witnessed the manifestations and demonstrations of the Holy Spirit, just like in the Book of Acts. I have been privileged to dream dreams and see visions. I am a God-possessed man, and I enjoy it very much. It strikes me as funny that people say it's not for today, but I am actually witnessing all of it.

JOHN 14:26	The Comforter
ACTS 1:8	The power to be a Christian
ROMANS 8:14	To be fathered

1. The Anointing   Yoke-destroying, burden-lifting
2. Guidance
3. Energy and Zeal
4. The Gifts
5. The Fruit   The reason Vickie and I live so happily.

The Gifts and Manifestations

1 CORINTHIANS 12:7-11

Revelatory Gifts

- Word of Wisdom
- Word of Knowledge
- Discerning of Spirits

Power Gifts

- Special Faith
- Working of Miracles
- Gifts of Healing

Utterance Gifts

- Prophecy
- Tongues – divers kinds
- Interpretation of Tongues

The Enabler

Demonstrations, Manifestations, Revelations, Illuminations

JOHN 14:16

1. **ACTS 1:8**
   - Power from the Holy Ghost.

2. **LUKE 24:49**
   - Wait for the power from on high.

3. **ACTS 10:38**
   - Jesus was anointed with the Holy Spirit and power.

4. **LUKE 4:14**
   - Jesus returned in power and Spirit.

5. **ROMANS 15:19**
   - Signs and wonders through the power of the Holy Spirit convinced many.

6. **JOHN 14:26**
   - Teach you all things.
   - Bring all things to your remembrance.

7. **JOHN 16:7-13**
   - Guide you into all truth.

8. **1 JOHN 2:27**
   • Anointing in you teaches you so you understand.

9. **ROMANS 9:1**
   • The Holy Spirit helps us tell the truth.

10. **LUKE 4:1**
    • Jesus was led by the Spirit.

11. **ROMANS 8:14**
    • We are to be led by the Spirit.

12. **ACTS 10:1-11**
    • Trances and visions given by God's great Spirit.

13. **ACTS 16:6-10**
    • Supernatural Guidance – Man from Macedonia

14. **JOHN 14:26**
    • Holy Spirit to be the Comforter, Consoler, Intercessor.

15. **JOHN 15:26**
    • He is to testify of Jesus.

16. **JOHN 16:13-14**
    • Guide you into all truth.
    • Show you things to come.
    • Glorify Jesus

17. **JOHN 20:22**
    • Born again – Born of the Spirit

18. **ACTS 2:2-4**
    • He came.
    • They spoke in tongues, etc.

19. **ACTS 2:39**
    • It's for YOU and EVERYONE.

Secret #14

DISCIPLINE

ACTS 20:28

Taking Heed to Myself

1 TIMOTHY 4:16

Discipline and Training

- Especially training of the mind or character.
- The training effect of experience, misfortune, or other happenings.
- A trained condition of order and obedience.

1. **I made up my mind, once and for all.**
2. **I create good habits.**
   - They don't just happen.
   - Decide and execute.
3. **I keep things in biblical order.**
4. **I keep things in order at home.**
   - Clothes
   - Keys
   - Etc.
5. **I keep things in order with family.**
6. **I have a disciplined exercise program.**
7. **I have a doctor-monitored, well-balanced program of vitamins, minerals, and trace minerals.**
8. **I keep my body in a state of alkalinity, not just hydration.**
9. **I sleep.**

The Holy Spirit Gives Us Power Over These

1. God complex (you're in charge)
2. Greed
3. Lust
4. Strife
5. Selfishness
6. Pride

Seven Things You Have Dominion Over in This Life

1. The devil himself
2. Demon spirits
3. Sickness and symptoms
4. Doubts
5. Fears
6. Sin, strongholds, and bondage
7. Mammon, poverty, lack, and debt

Create Patterns in Your Life

1. Go to church.
2. Study your Bible.
3. Pray.
4. Pray in tongues.
5. Tithe.
6. Give.

2 TIMOTHY 2:3

Thou therefore endure hardness, as a good **soldier**
of Jesus Christ.

2 TIMOTHY 2:4

No man that warreth entangleth himself with the affairs
of *this* life; that he may please him who hath chosen him
to be a **soldier**.

You are a soldier of the cross. Get in your rank and file, and stay there.
Stick to it. Improvise. Adapt. Overcome!

Deal with yourself. Judge (examine) yourself. Take charge of your flesh,
and overcome your weaknesses.

CONCLUSION

At the writing of this book, I am 65 years old. I am now in my forty-first year of ministry, preaching the uncompromised Word of God to the entire world. I dated Vickie for 5 years, and we have been married 47 years. My kids and some of my grandkids are grown, and I am now a great-grandfather.

I am still very strong and very healthy. I plan to conclude my story one day as I live on at least another 30 years and tell you how my final phase of ministry was carried out. Look for *God Possessed Part 2* in the future!

PRAYER OF SALVATION

YOU CAN BE SAVED FROM ETERNAL DAMNATION!

Get God's help now, in this life. All you have to do is humble your heart, believe in Christ's work at Calvary for you, and pray this prayer:

Dear Heavenly Father,

I know that I have sinned and fallen short of Your expectations of me. I have come to realize that I cannot run my own life. I do not want to continue the way I've been living, neither do I want to face an eternity of torment and damnation.

I know that the wages of sin is death, but I can be spared from this through the gift of the Lord Jesus Christ. I believe that He died for me, and I receive His provision now. I will not be ashamed of Him, and I will tell all my friends and family members that I have made this wonderful decision.

Dear Lord Jesus,

Come into my heart now and live in me and be my Savior, Master, and Lord. I will do my very best to chase after You and learn Your ways by submitting to a pastor, reading my Bible, going to a church that preaches about You, and keeping sin out of my life.

I also ask You to give me the power to be healed from all sickness and disease and to deliver me from those things that have me bound.

I love You and thank You for having me, and I am eagerly looking forward to a long, beautiful relationship with You.

Amen.

OTHER PRODUCT BY MARK BARCLAY PUBLICATIONS

BOOKS

Avoiding the Pitfalls of Familiarity

This book is a scriptural study about the most devastating sin in the body of Christ today. The truths in this book will make you aware of this excess familiarity and reveal to you some counterattacks.

Beware of Seducing Spirits

This is not a book on demonology. It is a book about people who are close to being in trouble with God because of demonic activity or fleshly bad attitudes.

Building a Supernatural Church

A step-by-step guide to pioneering, organizing, and establishing a local church.

Enduring Hardness

God has designed a program for His saints that will cause each one to be enlarged and victorious. This book will challenge your stability, steadfastness, courage, endurance, and determination and will motivate you to become a fighter.

How to Always Reap a Harvest

In this book, Dr. Barclay explains the principles that help us to be successful and fruitful. It explains how to live a better life, become far more productive, and enjoy a full harvest.

How to Avoid Shipwreck

A book of preventives, helping people to remain strong and full of faith. You will be strengthened by this book as you learn how to anchor your soul.

How to Relate to Your Pastor

It is very important in these last days that God's people understand the office of pastor. As we put into practice these principles, the Church will grow in numbers and also increase its vision for the world.

How to Survive a Betrayal

Often the most difficult thing to deal with concerning betrayal is the fact that it almost always comes from the people you love, trust, or respect. This amazing book will help you press on, recover, and once again become productive when a betrayal strikes your heart.

Improving Your Performance

Every leader everywhere needs to read this book. It will help tremendously in the organization and unity of your ministry and work force.

Man Maker—Insights on Having a Great Marriage

I was interviewed by the famous sportscaster, Mr. Pat Summerall, as one of his American Success Stories. Pat asked me for my secret to success. Without hesitation, I reported with great accuracy the passion in my heart. My answer? I had met two beings in my life who changed me forever. The first is the Lord Jesus Christ. The second is my wife Vickie. I humbly confess that without these two wonderful beings in my life, I would still be a drunk and a total loser—that is, if I were even still alive.

Preachers of Righteousness

As you read this book, you will be both edified and challenged to not only do the work of the ministry but to do it with humility, honesty, and godliness.

The Real Truth About Tithing
With the extremely fast-paced lifestyle of these last days, it leaves little time to thoroughly study God's Word. When you finish this book, you will be fully equipped and informed to tithe properly and accurately. All of your tithing questions should be answered. Your life will never be the same.

Sheep, Goats, and Wolves
A scriptural yet practical explanation of human behavior in our local churches and how church leaders and members can deal with each other.

Six Ways to Check Your Leadings
It seems that staying in the main flow of Jesus is one of the most difficult things for believers to do, including some preachers. Many people border on mysticism and a world of fantasy. God is not a goofy god. He doesn't intend for His people to be goofy either. This book reveals the six most valuable New Testament ways to live in accuracy and stay perfectly on course. This book is a must for living in these last days.

The Making of a Man of God
In this book you'll find some of the greatest yet simplest insights to becoming a man or woman of God and launching your ministry with accuracy and credibility. The longevity of your ministry will be enhanced by these truths.

The Missing Red Letters
There is nothing you will face in this life that is not covered by the Holy Scriptures. In these powerful Words of Christ (the red letters), every issue of life is addressed in one way or another. You will see that Jesus covered family, wages, violations, the law, supply, friends, your neighbor, and yes, even your enemies... and much more.

The Sin of Lawlessness

Lawlessness always challenges authority and ultimately is designed to hurt people. This book will convict those who are in lawlessness and warn those who could be future victims. It will help your life and straighten your walk with Him.

The Remnant Church

God has always had a people and will always have a people. Dr. Barclay speaks of the upcoming revival and how we can be those who are alive and remain when our Master returns.

Things You Need for the Day Ahead

This book was written to alert everyone (sinner and saint) to the coming perils, calamities, and filth that human power will not be able to overcome. Much of the future will be affected by holy wars and the terrible elements attached to them. This will be a prelude to the entry of the antichrist. Those who cling to truth and the Lord Jesus Christ will make it—some as survivors and some as conquerors. They will endure to the end.

Walking With God

A handbook for the Spirit-filled life, this book is sure to stir you on in pursuing more of the things of the Spirit. It also makes a great gift for those who don't understand the Spirit-filled life, giving thorough explanation, mixed with real experience, regarding the following topics: The Ministry of the Holy Spirit; The Holy Spirit in Action; No Mere Man; Holy Spirit Baptism; The Anointing; Led by the Spirit; How to Check Your Leadings; The Eyes of Your Spirit; The Armor of God; The Fruit of the Spirit; The Gifts of God; How to Develop in the Gifts; On Fire for God; Making the Holy Spirit Your Best Friend!

201

Warring Mental Warfare

Every person is made up of body, soul, and spirit and fights battles on each of these three fronts. The war against your soul (made up of your mind, will, and emotions) is real and as lethal as spiritual and natural enemies. This book will help you identify, war against, and defeat the enemies of your soul. Learn to quit coping with depression, anxiety, fear, and other hurts, and begin conquering those things now!

What About Death?

In this book, Brother Barclay deals with the enemy (death) and how to overcome it. He also explains what the Bible says about life after death. Many people have no real Bible knowledge on this subject and therefore are unsure about it all the days of their lives.

MINIBOOKS

Basic Christian Handbook

This book contains basic doctrines that are simple yet necessary to every Christian's walk with God. It will be a vital help to new converts in the Kingdom.

Have You Seen This Person Lately?

Did you once serve the Lord actively and fervently, but now you have cooled off? Are you now serving Him and want to assure that you will never backslide? Do you have family or friends who are backslidden or unchurched? Then this book is for you! Its contents will help you or someone you care about find the way home.

The Captain's Mantle

Something happened in the cave Adullum. Find out how 400 distressed, indebted, and discontented men came out of that cave as one of the most awesome armies in history!

MANUALS

Ministry of Helps

Ministry of Helps is a companion manual to the *Minister's Manual* and was written to help pastors, ministers, administrators, and other leaders to establish a strong and effective ministry of helps in the local church. Topics include training and qualifications, organization, communications, church leadership, having church, and more.

Minister's Manual

Minister's Manual is a companion manual to *Ministry of Helps* and was written with the specific needs of ministers in mind. Topics include ethics, governments, administration, building a ministry of helps, the local church, sacraments, pastoring the local church, executives, protocol, the supernatural and the practical, and more.

SERIES

How to Study Your Bible

In this powerful series, Brother Barclay offers three teachings on this vital topic. The first two titles cover how to study your Bible personally and at church. The third message offers insight into tools to help you study your Bible.

SUPERNATURAL MINISTRIES TRAINING INSTITUTE (SMTI)

"Building Believers for Ministry"

SMTI is a contemporary ministry training institute, specializing in spiritual Bible training—building, developing, and equipping believers with the Scriptures to function supernaturally in all areas of ministry. SMTI presents the uncompromised, practical, life-adjusting Word of God in a straightforward, understandable format that is applicable for a wide range of individuals (lay people as well as full-time ministers). SMTI designs and presents scriptural curriculum in a way that builds character, imparts vision, and provides insight about the end times—causing believers and churches to flourish and courageously climax the ages.

CURRICULUM

The SMTI curriculum includes three different courses of study. Each course is designed to be completed in a nine-month period (31 weeks of teachings). All classes are taught by Mark T. Barclay.

Supernatural Helps

Supernatural Helps is designed to build character, help define and perfect the call on an individual's life, and develop supportive ministries in the local church.

Ministerial Practicalities

Ministerial Practicalities will provide practical training about the local church, administration, legalities, ceremonies, executive ethics, and wisdom to perform with excellence in the ministry.

Advanced Survival Techniques

Advanced Survival Techniques is designed to help the end-time leaders and believers in dealing with the crucial matters of life and ministry.